T0316781

GOD'S RESISTANCE

God's Resistance

Mobilizing Faith to Defend Immigrants

Brad Christerson,
Alexia Salvatierra,
Robert Chao Romero, *and*
Nancy Wang Yuen

NEW YORK UNIVERSITY PRESS

New York

NEW YORK UNIVERSITY PRESS
New York
www.nyupress.org

Please contact the Library of Congress for Cataloging-in-Publication data.
ISBN: 9781479816415 (hardback)
ISBN: 9781479816422 (paperback)
ISBN: 9781479816446 (library ebook)
ISBN: 9781479816439 (consumer ebook)

This book is printed on acid-free paper, and its binding materials are chosen for strength and durability. We strive to use environmentally responsible suppliers and materials to the greatest extent possible in publishing our books.

Manufactured in the United States of America

10 9 8 7 6 5 4 3 2 1

Also available as an ebook

To all people forced to leave their homes and countries for the safety and well-being of themselves and their families. May God's protection and blessing be upon you.

CONTENTS

Mobilizing

This book is a labor of love for all four of us because we are not only academic social scientists but also participants in the movement we describe and analyze. This is somewhat unusual for an academic book. One of us, Alexia Salvatierra, has been a nationally recognized figure in the faith-based immigrant rights movement for over forty years. Widely known as the *Madrina*, or godmother, of the movement, she participated in the Sanctuary Movement of the 1980s, cofounded the New Sanctuary Movement beginning in the early 2000s, and is a key leader in the current iteration of the movement that we analyze in the book. She played a role in founding or leading a number of principal movement organizations at different times, including Clergy and Laity United for Economic Justice (CLUE), the Evangelical Immigration Table, and Matthew 25 / Mateo 25. The rest of us have been connected sporadically to a number of groups, including Matthew 25 / Mateo 25, CLUE, LA Voice, and We Care, as volunteers. We personally know the leaders of other key organizations in the movement, have participated in numerous actions, some of which are recorded and analyzed in this book, and have deep, personal connections to numerous vulnerable immigrants, some of whose stories are highlighted in these pages.

This personal involvement means that we are not simply playing the role of "objective" outside observers (a problematic concept to begin with) but rather are "participant observers" with a personal stake in the work. Our location as participants has allowed us access to key movement leaders, lay volunteers, and the vulnerable immigrants who are most affected by the work. Our trust relationships with these individuals have afforded us access to candid, behind-the-scenes conversations, stories, decisions, real-time experiences as actions and events unfolded, and insights as insiders that would be unavailable to outsiders. In addition to our participation in the movement, however, we conducted over forty formal, in-depth interviews with immigrants, leaders, and laypeople, many of whom we had had no previous personal connection with, between 2018 and 2020. We used rigorous coding methods to analyze these interviews and to understand our findings theoretically. Thus, we have employed a combination of participant observation and qualitative, in-depth interview analysis to arrive at the theoretical conclusions we offer in this book.

We acknowledge that our location as participant observers with a personal stake in the work influences our interpretations of our findings, but the trust relationships, insider access, firsthand accounts of decisions and actions, and personal real-time experiences provide a powerful advantage compared to outside observers with no personal experience or connection to the work. We acknowledge that our position as both participants and analysts of this movement might bias our findings—for example, we may have personal experiences that might lead us to focus on particular organizational strategies, obstacles, or dynamics as more important, while potentially neglecting others that we have had less contact with. Yet we have tried to correct for this by interviewing leaders, lay participants, and immigrant informants whom we had little to no contact with as part of the movement. We also acknowledge that we are all immersed in the movement from the perspective of our geographic location in Southern California, which affects our ability to see dynamics and strategies that may be more prominent elsewhere. Yet Dr. Salvatierra's history as a leader in the national movement has made us aware of those differences. We do not claim that our analysis is exhaustive or fully generalizable to other locations or movements. We do maintain, however, that our position as insiders in the Southern California faith-based movement for immigrant rights, and, in the case of Dr. Salvatierra, in the national movement, gives us rich analytical insights into the social dynamics of this movement that would not be available to outsiders.

In addition to our personal connection to the movement, another unique aspect of this project is that we are also a multidisciplinary group of academic researchers. Robert Chao Romero is a historian, Brad Christerson and Nancy Wang Yuen are sociologists, and Alexia Salvatierra is a scholar in religious/cultural studies. We are thus able to combine and incorporate the research methods and theoretical insights of all of our disciplines into our discussions and analysis in this book.

Our multidisciplinary training and combined methods of historical research, participant observation, and qualitative interview analysis have allowed us to write a somewhat unusual book. For example, Alexia Salvatierra's firsthand accounts and personal experiences as the Madrina of the movement are woven into the historical account of the faith-based movement for immigrant rights in chapter 1. Her deep firsthand understanding of the relationships between faith-based and secular advocacy organizations informs chapter 2's description of the institutional field of the immigrant rights movement. Rich descriptions of real-time firsthand experiences, extensive interview quotes, and theoretical concepts from our three disciplines are woven throughout the book.

Our analysis is centered on six case studies of faith-based organizations working to accompany, defend, and advocate for vulnerable immigrants in Southern California. We focused on organizations in this area because they are central to the national movement and because focusing on the one region in which we are all deeply embedded allowed for more in-depth analysis of the groups and their networks. Our six case studies explore the following organizations:

1) *Matthew 25 / Mateo 25*—a nonprofit organization led by Latina/o evangelical leaders that was formed immediately after the 2016 election. Its primary strategy is to create partnerships between evangelical immigrant congregations and nonimmigrant congregations to accompany, protect, and advocate for asylum seekers with the long-term goal of advocating for federal immigration reform.

2) *Clergy and Laity United for Economic Justice (CLUE)*—an interfaith, ecumenical organization cofounded by civil rights veteran Rev. James Lawson Jr. in Los Angeles in 1996. CLUE has been highly involved in advocating for immigrants for decades and was a lead organization in the New Sanctuary Movement in the 2000s. Its current primary modes of action are (a) documenting human rights abuses at immigration detention centers for use in legal challenges to Immigration and Customs Enforcement practices, (b) advocating for the release of individuals in immigration

detention, (c) providing temporary shelter and accompaniment for recently released detainees.

3) *United Methodist Welcoming Congregations Network*—a network of Methodist congregations providing resources for asylum seekers, undocumented immigrants, and unaccompanied minors at United Methodist Church congregation-based welcome centers, three in greater Los Angeles and one in northern San Diego County. These welcome centers offer (a) legal services and advocacy, (b) post-trauma counseling, (c) leadership development, and (d) educational assistance.

4) *We Care*—a nonprofit based in a Los Angeles Latina/o Baptist congregation that mobilizes a national network of congregations, individuals, legal aid organizations, and other faith-based non-profit organizations to sponsor, host, arrange legal assistance, and advocate for asylum seekers.

5) *Southern California Immigration Task Force of the Catholic Church*—a network of Catholic clergy and laypeople in the four-county region of Southern California providing legal advocacy and education for undocumented immigrants and advocating for immigration reform.

6) *La Voice*—a multifaith ecumenical organization that is part of the national Faith in Action network. Its current primary mode of action in the area of immigration is mobilizing congregations in its network for immigration policy reform at the state and local levels.

The goal of these case studies was to identify the role of faith in the strategies utilized by these organizations in promoting the well-being of immigrants and defending them from being harmed by immigration policy enforcement. In analyzing our data, we found that faith both enables and constrains the groups' ability to pursue their goals in powerful and unexpected ways.

The book is organized by first situating the current faith-based movement to defend and advocate for immigrants in historical context. The first chapter details the history of faith-based immigrant advocacy in the United States. The second chapter contextualizes the current faith-based movement within the larger U.S.-based movement for immigrant rights, mapping the field of influential organizations and their connections with each other. Chapters 3, 4, and 5 are centered on our case studies, analyzing the groups' strategies, successes, and obstacles as they mobilize faith to defend and advocate for immigrants. Chapter 3 focuses on the work of accompaniment—helping vulnerable immigrants access basic needs like housing, child care, medical care, food, and nonlegal logistical support as well as giving spiritual and emotional support to those seeking asylum. Chapter 4 analyzes the work of advocacy, including mobilizing for policy change, at the national, state, and local levels as well as supporting individual cases and class-action lawsuits against the federal government. Chapter 5 highlights the work of education, including teaching and training leaders in the practical tools of organizing and educating community members in how to advocate for themselves and resist the forces harming their families and communities.

We conclude the book by exploring the theoretical implications of our findings. Broadly, we conclude that faith both enables and constrains the work of organizing a resistance movement to defend immigrants and promote their well-being in the face of harmful government policies. More specifically, we connect these findings to recent theoretical advances in the study of religion in social movements, such as the power of spiritual capital in building community cultural wealth (Yosso 2005; Pérez Huber 2009; Park, Dizon, and Malcolm 2019), the power of religion as bridging social capital (Wood 2002), and the benefits of and obstacles created by multi-target religious social movements (Yukich 2013). We also connect our findings to more established theories showing the tendency of religion to legitimate authority and power and the effects of the domination of U.S. religion by European Americans and their religious institutions.

Though the volume may be unusually interdisciplinary, our aim is to leverage the strengths of our combined experiences, methods of analysis, and theoretical insights to pull back the veil on a dynamic and powerful movement and view it from different angles. Our goal has been to create a book that is not only theoretically interesting but also helpful for practitioners in ways that are politically, socially, and religiously transformative.

1

History

Pastor Luis Reyes[1] is a minister in the Assemblies of God denomination and has lived in the United States for more than two decades. At the age of eight, during the civil war in Guatemala, he was kidnapped by guerrillas. After five years in captivity, he escaped and fled to the United States as a child refugee. Luis eventually married a U.S. citizen and became the father of two beautiful U.S. citizen children. Although he has no criminal record, in July 2017 he was arrested and detained by Immigration and Customs Enforcement (ICE) during a periodic check-in with immigration officials.

In response to his arrest, a multicultural network of Christians rallied to his side under the leadership of Latina/o pastors from the Los Angeles area. These pastors, of various denominational and organizational affiliations, including American Baptist, Assemblies of God, Lutheran, Fuller Seminary's Centro Latino, and Matthew 25 / Mateo 25, included, among others, Melvin and Ada Valiente, Alexia Salvatierra, Sergio Navarrete, Carlos Rincon, Jack Miranda, and Jaime Lazaro. What made their organizing strategy unique was the fusion of pan-Latino cultural practices, Pentecostal spirituality, and nonviolence of heart and action. A week-long prayer and worship gathering was staged at ICE headquarters in downtown Los Angeles; letters incorporating scriptural references and Catholic social teachings were sent to the director of ICE; fasting and prayer chains were conducted from Los Angeles to South America; state, local, and federal legislators were petitioned; and stories of the case were featured in newspapers, on English-language cable news, and in Spanish-language media. All of the fourteen superintendents of the Spanish-speaking Assemblies of God districts across the United States came together in an unprecedented act of advocacy, which inspired the top international leader of the Assemblies of God to go to the White House on behalf of Pastor Reyes. Despite this advocacy, Pastor Luis remained in detention for over two months. After it seemed that all hope was lost and all avenues of advocacy had been exhausted, Pastor Luis was released from the Adelanto detention facility and reunited with his family on September 22, 2017.

Unbeknownst to most community members who participated in the national campaign to free Pastor Luis, their efforts were part of a century-old tradition of Latina/o faith-based immigrant organizing tracing back to the days of Jim Crow. As context for the study of faith-based organizations that have mobilized to protect immigrants in Southern California over the past decade, this chapter provides a brief history of such faith-based pro-immigrant movements in the United States, with special emphasis on the first Sanctuary Movement of the 1980s, the New Sanctuary Movement, and the specific contributions of the Latina/o immigrant community itself as active agents. Methodologically, this chapter is unique insofar as its periodization and analysis are structured upon the oral histories of Rev. Dr. Alexia Salvatierra, who has been an eyewitness, participant, and leader of the various sanctuary movements over the past four decades. As the Madrina of the faith-based immigrant rights movement in the United States, Salvatierra offers a firsthand and behind-the-scenes glimpse and understanding of the inner workings of the U.S. Sanctuary Movement. Dr. Salvatierra was a young member of one of the first congregations to declare sanctuary in 1980, a founding member of the New Sanctuary Movement in the 2000s, and an ongoing leader in the development of other faith-based approaches to the immigration crisis. This chapter contains personal stories that have stayed with her over the years and shaped her faith and approach to advocacy on behalf of immigrants.

In alignment with the analysis of religious studies scholars Lloyd Barba and Tatyana Castillo-Ramos (2021, 1–4), this chapter contests the classical narrative of the U.S. Sanctuary Movement as an "immigrant movement without immigrant leaders."

Early Efforts of Latina/o Faith-Based Immigrant Advocacy

The earliest efforts of Latina/o faith-based immigrant advocacy took place among Mexican American Catholic leaders of the Jim Crow era. According to Chicano historian Mario García, immigrant rights advocates including Alonso Perales and Cleofas Calleros drew upon their distinct Mexican American Catholicism and Christianity "as a form of resistance and affirmation to growing Anglo racism" and as a "way of organizing defense mechanisms . . . [and] asserting a sense of dignity and community" (García 2008, 56). Mexican American Catholic leaders of the Jim Crow era interpreted and filtered Catholic social teaching through their own ethnic identity and experiences and applied it to their civil rights struggles related to housing, education, health care, and politics.

Perales was born in Alice, Texas, in 1898 to a middle-class Mexican American family whose ancestral roots predated the U.S. conquest of the Southwest. Credited with having "una vision de profeta" (a vision of a prophet), he cofounded the League of United Latin American Citizens (LULAC) in 1929 (García 2008, 57–60). LULAC was the leading Mexican American civil rights organization of the era and played key roles in landmark civil rights cases such as *Hernandez v. Texas* (1954) and *Mendez v. Westminster* (1947). Perales worked as a lawyer, diplomat, and newspaper columnist and was also a veteran of the First World War.

Calleros was born in Chihuahua, Mexico, in 1896 and came to El Paso, Texas, in 1902. Known as the "apostle of the border," Calleros served for many years as head of the Bureau of Immigration of the National Catholic Welfare Conference (NCWC; García 2008, 59–62). The NCWC was created in 1919 and had as its goal the "unifying, coordinating, and organizing [of] the Catholic people of the United States in works of education, social welfare, immigration aid, and other activities" (García 2008, 62). Like Perales, Calleros also served in World War I and was a noted newspaper columnist. Similar to many important leaders of the Latina/o community, both then and now, Calleros was a self-educated "organic intellectual."

Drawing from Catholic social teachings, they fought for Mexican American rights to earn a living wage and live free from racial segregation. According to Calleros, Mexicans were never paid enough to survive, and Euro-American employees with equal or lesser experience were paid more by virtue of their racial background. In 1930 Calleros stated, "The employer believes that because of the mere fact he is a Mexican he is supposed to receive a smaller wage and is expected to live on less" (García 2008, 66). Perales emphasized the inherent equality of all human beings, regardless of race or ethnic background: "Equal in the trenches, but also equal in the factories, in the stores, in the schools, in the churches, in the restaurants, in the barbershops, in the theaters, and everywhere else" (García 2008, 73).

In the 1960s and 1970s, following in the religious-based civil rights footsteps of Perales and Calleros, other faith-rooted Latina/o immigrant rights movements and organizations sprang into action. César Chávez and Dolores Huerta struggled for the rights of immigrant farmworkers. Padres Asociados para Derechos Religiosos, Educativos, y Sociales (Association of Fathers for Religious, Educational, and Social Rights; PADRES), together with Las Hermanas (The Sisters) and Católicos Por La Raza (Catholics for the Race), strategically confronted the racist institutional practices of the U.S. Roman Catholic Church (Martinez 2010; Medina 2004; García 2008). Most movement scholars have ignored the centrality of Christian spirituality in the lives of Chávez and Huerta and the broader farmworkers movement. Chávez and Huerta fused popular Mexican religious symbols and practices—such as La Virgen de Guadalupe, *peregrinacion* (pilgrimage), and fasting—with Catholic social teaching, leading to the first successful unionization of farmworkers in U.S. history. Speaking of the central role of spirituality in his activism, Chávez once declared, "Today I don't think I could base my will to struggle on cold economics or on some political doctrine. I don't think there would be enough to sustain me. For me, the base must be faith" (Romero 2020, 121). PADRES, Las Hermanas, and Catolicos Por La Raza challenged entrenched race-based discriminatory practices of the U.S. Catholic Church against Mexican immigrants, including segregated seating, the dearth of Chicano priests and bishops, the patriarchal structure of the Church, and the lack of institutional support for the farmworkers' movement.

Thus, the first Sanctuary Movement of the 1980s did not emerge in a historical vacuum but represented an extension of this rich legacy of Latina/o organizing in the Southwest.

The First Sanctuary Movement

Three decades after the religious advocacy efforts of Perales, Calleros, and LULAC, state-sponsored violence in Central America gave rise to a new religious uprising among Latinas/os in the United States—the

Sanctuary Movement. During the 1970s and 1980s, El Salvadoran and Guatemalan military forces, in cahoots with oligarchic elites, initiated violent counterinsurgency campaigns to crush all political challenges to their ruling authority. Reports indicate that death squads and military organizations killed seventy-five thousand people in El Salvador and more than two hundred thousand in Guatemala (Buergenthal 1994; Rothenberg 2016). Military and paramilitary forces beheaded their foes, skinned people alive, slit throats, and even ripped unborn children from their mothers' wombs. Murdered corpses were dumped in village squares as warnings to potential sympathizers. In Guatemala, armed forces focused largely upon the indigenous populations of regions such as El Quiché, Huehuetenango, and El Petén. One missionary labeled these murderous campaigns of Central America a "hermeneutic of death" (Cunningham 1995, 21).

The Guatemalan and Salvadoran governments' brutal campaigns were carried out with U.S. political, military, and economic assistance. Moreover, the brutality was led by officers and soldiers trained at the U.S. Army School of the Americas in Columbus, Georgia. U.S. economic and military intervention during this era was part of a larger project of neocolonialism in Latin America, with roots tracing to the nineteenth and early twentieth centuries. U.S. neocolonial expansion was established by a combination of direct military intervention, treaties, and diplomatic policies such as the Monroe Doctrine (1823), the Platt Amendment (1901), Dollar Diplomacy (1909–1913), and the Good Neighbor Policy (1933) (Crandall and Crandall 2021, xi, xii).

U.S. military intervention, coupled with such diplomatic policies, ensured U.S. economic dominance as it allowed for private U.S. corporations such as the United Fruit Company to control millions of hectares of land in such countries as El Salvador, Guatemala, Honduras, and Cuba. These U.S. corporations partnered with Latin American oligarchs to create highly profitable schemes of agricultural export at the expense of the landless and impoverished masses who were exploited as cheap labor. Although this approach allowed for economic growth and modernization at a national level in some countries, it did not translate into economic development and prosperity for most people. The economic analysis explaining this neocolonial relationship with the United States, originating from Latin American scholars, became known as dependency theory (Cardoso and Faletto 1979). As a consistent pattern throughout the twentieth century, U.S. military and political intervention accompanied any attempts to disrupt such neocolonial patterns, sometimes through the violent overthrow of democratically elected governments. During the Cold War years, leaders justified such military involvement in Latin America with the threat of communism (Barba and Castillo-Ramos 2019, 19). The violent U.S.-backed civil wars in El Salvador and Guatemala must be understood in light of this larger historical context.

In the 1970s and 1980s, a small but vocal minority of Roman Catholic and Protestant lay leaders, nuns, and priests challenged the government-sanctioned violence and underlying socioeconomic disparities in Central America from a liberation theology perspective. Base Christian communities (small groups of around twenty people studying the Bible and applying its calls for justice to their communities) were established among the people to raise the spiritual and political consciousness of their members and mobilize against government violence, poverty, and repression. As part of these efforts, liberationist clergy publicly denounced the landowning elite who monopolized agricultural landholdings to the detriment of the rural masses. Some, such as Archbishop Oscar Romero, maintained strict methods of pacifism. Others joined the military efforts of guerrilla forces such as the Farabundo Martí National Liberation Front (FMLN). In an attempt to squelch popular support for the FMLN, death squads targeted those who supported farming cooperatives as well as priests, nuns, and anyone perceived as sympathetic to the FMLN. Many priests, nuns, and religious workers, among whom Oscar Romero is the most remembered, were martyred in successive waves of violence.

In February 1977, precisely because of his conservative reputation, Romero was installed as Archbishop of San Salvador. The murder of his close friend, Jesuit priest Rutilio Grande, one month later, however, became a turning point that led to his political and spiritual concientization. From that point on, Romero realized that neutrality in the face of murder and repression was no longer possible in El Salvador. Christ is the God of life, so to follow him requires his followers—of all epochs—to struggle against the oppression of the poor: "We see with great clarity that here neutrality is impossible. . . . And here what is most fundamental about the faith is given expression in history: either we believe in a God of life, or we serve the idols of death" (quoted in Romero 2020, 66). Through weekly sermons broadcast over national radio, pastoral letters, and public talks, Romero decried the torture, murders, and disappearances perpetrated by the El Salvadoran totalitarian state. He fought with little support from the Vatican and in the face of opposition from many of his fellow bishops who accused him of mixing religion with politics. Invoking the spiritual truths of liberation theology, Romero embraced the doctrine of the preferential option for the poor and declared that, in the face of murder and exploitation, God takes the side of the Salvadoran masses: "A church that does not join the poor, in order to speak out from the side of the poor against the injustices committed against them, is not the true church of Jesus Christ" (Romero 2004). In the end, Romero was martyred for his prophetic Christian witness. On March 24, 1980, he was assassinated while administering Mass in the chapel of the Divina Providencia Hospital. Nearly forty years later, on October 14, 2018, he was declared a saint.

In response to such horrific state-sponsored violence, over one million Salvadorans, Guatemalans, and other Central Americans fled as refugees to the United States in the seventies and eighties (Barba and Castillo-Ramos 2019, 19; García 2018, 85; Cadava 2013, 199). Because of its complicity with the oligarchic governments that were perpetuating the violence, however, the U.S. government denied asylum to virtually all who arrived at its doors. This was because granting asylum would be akin to an admission that such asylum seekers were fleeing political violence funded by the Reagan administration (Barba and Castillo-Ramos 2019, 19). In virtually all cases, the denial of asylum was declared without even due process. In fact, only 2 to 3 percent of Salvadorans and Guatemalans who sought asylum were granted it during the 1980s (Chinchilla, Hamilton, and Loucky 2009, 108). The rejection of asylum was justified on the grounds that Central American migrants were not political refugees but instead undocumented immigrants simply in search of economic opportunity. This refusal of asylum ran counter to the Refugee Act of 1980 and international law. According to the Refugee Act, it was illegal for the U.S. government to deny asylum to any refugee whose life or freedom was threatened because of persecution based on race, religion, nationality, political opinion, or membership in a social group, within the confines of an overall cap on the number of refugees. In refusing asylum to hundreds of thousands of Central Americans, the United States violated its own law because they were fleeing political violence in their countries of origin and to send them back home would be to deport them to death.

Romero's lived example of "the preferential option for the poor" inspired many from *el otro lado*. Among those touched by his message were the hundreds of thousands of Central American migrants, clergy, and allies who formed the U.S. Sanctuary Movement during the 1980s.

The Sanctuary Movement officially began on March 24, 1982, the second anniversary of the martyrdom of Archbishop Oscar Romero. Building upon the foundation of the civil rights activism of Isabel Garcia and Guadalupe Castillo of the Manzo Area Council (Cadava 2013; Barba and Castillo-Ramos 2021), on that day the Southside Presbyterian Church of Tucson publicly declared itself a "sanctuary" for Central American migrants:

> We are writing to inform you that the Southside Presbyterian Church will publicly violate the Immigration and Nationality Act Section 274(a). We have declared our church as a "sanctuary" for undocumented refugees from Central America . . . we believe that justice and mercy require that people of conscience actively assert our God-given right to aid anyone fleeing from persecution and murder. The current administration of U.S. law prohibits us from sheltering these refugees from Central America. Therefore, we believe the administration of the law to be immoral as well as illegal. (Barba and Castillo-Ramos 2021, 7).

Following this Tucson Declaration, spearheaded by pastor John Fife, Quaker rancher Jim Corbett, and the Tucson Ecumenical Council, the Sanctuary Movement quickly spread throughout the United States. In addition to Arizona, central hubs were established in Chicago, the San Francisco Bay Area, and Los Angeles. Hilary Cunningham (1995, 13) has defined the Sanctuary Movement thusly:

> This movement can be defined as a religiopolitical coalition that began as a network of churches and synagogues that decided to offer "safe haven" or "sanctuary" to Central American fugitives denied political asylum by

the U.S. Immigration and Naturalization Service (INS). . . . At its height in 1986–1987 it spanned Mexico, the United States, and Canada, included more than four hundred religious congregations, and claimed between sixty and seventy thousands participants.

As reflected in this definition, the Sanctuary Movement was based upon a coalition of Central American migrants, Mexican, U.S., and Canadian allies, together with predominantly white churches, synagogues, and Latina/o congregations. Members of the movement housed and sheltered migrants and protected them from deportation, lobbied for legislative reform, and even operated a transnational underground railroad involving Central America, Mexico, Canada, and the United States (Cadava 2013, 202).

As is common with many social justice movements, the Sanctuary Movement also experienced conflict within its membership related to leadership structure, goals, and political approach (Cunningham 1995, 38–39; Lorentzen 1991, 53). Inspired by Protestant, Congregationalist, and Quaker polities, Tucson leaders supported decision-making processes based upon localized consensus. In contrast, the Chicago stream (largely composed of Catholic participants) favored greater structure with an elected board setting goals and policy on the national level (García 2006, 102). Sanctuary workers also diverged with respect to how they viewed the fundamental nature of their work. Some believed that their efforts constituted civil disobedience, while others characterized their efforts as a civil initiative. From the perspective of the latter, it was the government, not the sanctuary workers themselves, that was disobeying both civil and moral law. Therefore, it was the responsibility of sanctuary workers to force a change in government policy (García 2006, 208).

Finally, leaders of the Sanctuary Movement also experienced persecution by the federal government. In 1985, sixteen Arizona Sanctuary workers were indicted on criminal charges for their work with the underground railroad (Cadava 2013, 205; Chinchilla, Hamilton, and Loucky 2009). Their charges included transporting, concealing, and harboring undocumented immigrants (Cunningham 1995, 44). Contrary to having a chilling effect, however, the Arizona arrests brought greater national attention to the movement as well as increased support by interfaith leaders of the U.S. religious community including the National Council of Churches, Roman Catholic bishops, and the Conference of American Rabbis. The Sanctuary Movement flourished under persecution and grew to 250 congregations, cities, and university campuses by the middle of 1985 and to 420 by 1987 (Chinchilla, Hamilton, and Loucky 2009, 107).

Although valuable studies of the Sanctuary Movement have been produced over the years, one critique is that they in general overlook the agency of Central American migrants and the role that U.S. Latina/o Christians played in the movement. As Barba and Castillo-Ramos (2019) have argued, however, Latina/o leadership in the original Sanctuary Movement was actually robust and widespread. Latina/o leaders exercised active agency but often chose to remain out of the limelight as a deliberate strategy in order to avoid arrest and deportation. The time has now come to tell their stories: "If we continue to ignore their work and fail to record the current leaders in critical moments such as now, we run the risk again of perpetuating a story that neglects not only individual people, but also broader understandings of leadership as maternal, as resistance, as subterfuge, as non-white. . . . When we continue to advance this myth . . . we unintentionally silence the stories of Latinx and immigrant leaders" (Barba and Castillo-Ramos 2021, 22).

In support of Barba and Castillo-Ramos's strong contention, the following firsthand account of Alexia Salvatierra highlights the role of Latina/o immigrant agency in the Sanctuary Movement. A young organizer in Berkeley at the time of the original Sanctuary Movement, Salvatierra peels back the curtain and offers personal glimpses into the role of Central American migrant leadership. Her oral history also sheds light on the contested beginnings of the Sanctuary Movement and the ecumenism and transnationalism that characterized those organizing efforts. She also discusses the theological and political differences that distinguished the two main movement streams, in Tucson and Chicago, and the important faith understandings of migrant leaders.

The Sanctuary Movement: A Firsthand Account

Alexia Salvatierra discusses the beginnings of the Sanctuary Movement in the paragraphs below:

The birth of the 1980s Sanctuary Movement is recorded in multiple books and articles. As in the four biblical Gospel accounts of the life of Jesus, the stories overlap, match, don't match—but they are all testimonies to the power of unjust suffering to move religious believers to risky action. The courage and sacrifice narratives of the movement are not only stories about the activities of North American allies; they are also stories about the asylum-seekers from Central America who dared to challenge a massive system to hear their voices and respond to their plight.

In 1980, Rev. John Fife, a tall blond pastor who looks like the Hollywood version of a cowboy, drove by the detention center in Tucson. Looking up, he saw a sheet hanging on the fence. The writing on the sheet looked like human blood. The letters spelled out "Ayudanos por el amor de Dios." He swung into the parking lot and demanded to be let in to visit the detainees. Rev. Fife is hard to refuse; he was able to speak to the Central Americans responsible for the sign and was introduced to their predicament. His first response was to find legal assistance and bail for them. It was only months later that he, and his other clergy allies, realized that legal assistance was insufficient; the system was rigged against them (Fife 2008).

As noted earlier, Southside Presbyterian Church in Tucson, John Fife's congregation, declared itself the first sanctuary church for Central American refugees on March 24, 1982, the second anniversary of the martyrdom of Archbishop Oscar Romero.

Jose came from San Salvador.[1] He had been a student activist when a number of his friends began to disappear. Bodies were found with clear evidence of torture; others were never found. Jose was part of a base Christian community and one of the students recruited to help as pastoral agents with base community organizing. The community was full of faith, deeply inspired by their growing conviction that God was with them in their struggle for justice. They fought for electricity and water for their neighborhoods, for land reform, for human rights. They had begun to chalk up some wins. Then Archbishop Oscar Romero was assassinated. Carrying a Bible in public became dangerous. Jose chose to run to the United States. However, he did not leave his activism behind. He could have slipped into the shadows of the sizeable undocumented community in the United States but instead became an active part of the Sanctuary Movement, sharing his story, speaking in churches, taking leadership at the Oakland Catholic Worker in their Sanctuary activities—potentially endangering not only his own life and future but also his family back home.

Jose's leadership, rooted in the passion and courage of faith, was not unusual. At University Lutheran Chapel in Berkeley, an early Sanctuary church, home to pastor Gus Schultz, who was ultimately indicted for his involvement in the movement, asylum seekers were part of the decision-making process.

The faith sector of the liberation movements in Central America, which helped to guide the U.S. movement, is commonly perceived to be solely Roman Catholic, but it was actually ecumenical. Bishop Medardo Gomez of the Lutheran Church of El Salvador was in the United States to help with wider church education for the Sanctuary Movement when the Jesuits associated with Romero were murdered. His church leaders begged him to stay in safety in the United States, but he chose instead to return to El Salvador. Upon his return, he discovered that the soldiers who had come to his cathedral had taken a cross that had been used at Lent as a canvas for the members of the congregation to declare their individual sins and those of the people—they called it a subversive cross. The cross had the words "torture," "violence," "disappearance," and "assassination" written on it. He invited the ambassadors of various Scandinavian countries and the press to accompany him to military headquarters, where he demanded the return of the cross. After he waited for several hours, the cross was given back. Bishop Gomez then placed the cross on the wall of the cathedral with a plaque underneath that read, "The Subversive Cross." Bishop Gomez's testimony had a major impact on Lutheran support within the United States for the Sanctuary Movement (Gomez 2013).

Rev. Shultz was intimately involved with the Share Foundation, led by Eileen Purcell, which was in regular communication with movement leaders in Central America about strategy. This connection between Central American leaders and U.S. Sanctuary leaders was not publicly acknowledged in order to avoid political charges in the United States that the Sanctuary Movement was being led by "communists" in Central America.

Everyone involved with the Sanctuary Movement took risks. The Reagan administration painted refugees as communists or economic migrants and their allies as dupes of communists. Its determination to prosecute the Sanctuary Movement was fierce, as illustrated by the following incident.

The Berkeley Emergency Food Project, housed at University Lutheran Chapel, served meals to a number of mentally ill unhoused individuals. At one point, several of the unhoused regulars began reporting that FBI agents were coming to meals disguised as unhoused people. These reports were ignored by the leaders of the project. Then the church office was broken into, reportedly by two unhoused people, but the only objects taken were Sanctuary Movement files. The federal administration ultimately succeeded in infiltrating the Sanctuary Movement, and a number of leaders went on trial in 1985. Two U.S. leaders, Jack Elder and Stacy Merkel, ultimately went to prison for their role in transporting asylum seekers across state lines. Six others who were indicted received lesser penalties. Although leaders were indicted and sentenced, the public trials provided an opportunity for faith leaders to communicate their biblical and theological case to a listening public.

In spite of the relatively small number of convictions, North American Sanctuary leaders lived for years in fear of prosecution and many Central American leaders feared deportation. Most asylum seekers exhibited symptoms of PTSD, which were severe for some of them. An asylum seeker living in our house died from a bicycle accident, which I felt was part of a larger pattern of recklessness that had set in as the months dragged on. However, the solidarity between asylum seekers who shared a profound Christian faith acted as an ongoing source of healing and resilience for many, as did their continuance of the same faith-based activism that they had practiced in Central America.

Ironically, federal prosecution may have also preserved the unity of the movement. When the news broke of the indictments of Elder, Merkel, and the others, Sanctuary Movement leaders were meeting in Chicago, where leaders from the border states and those from the Midwest were struggling with serious disagreements about the primary goal of the movement and its implications for who would be helped and how. Border leaders, particularly in Texas, were committed to providing hospitality to all Central Americans, including Nicaraguans. Leaders from other parts of the country were concerned that the message for the United States to stop supporting Central American regimes violating human rights would be muddied and confused by Nicaraguans' stories. The attack on their movement by the government caused Sanctuary Movement leaders from all over the country to unite in defense.

The Role of Faith in the Sanctuary Movement

The power of the biblical perspective on the refugees and their situation, as described by Dr. Salvatierra above, shifted the perception of the public in ways that significantly contributed to the movement's ultimate victories. The Sanctuary Movement's lobbying efforts led to, among other victories, the termination of funding for Central American regimes, the establishment of Temporary Protected Status (TPS) for Central Americans as part of the Immigration Act of 1990, and a seminal court case (*American Baptist Churches v. Thornburgh*, 1991) that changed the policy and practices of the asylum system.

The Sanctuary Movement was founded by Central American migrants themselves (along with their U.S.-based allies) who reflected upon biblical scriptures in light of their own experiences of injustice in Central America and the United States. They were followers of Jesus— Catholic and Protestant—long before stepping foot in the United States, and many were familiar with liberation theology. They had their own living faith and knew that God cared for them in their mistreatment and oppression. Reflecting upon the Bible, they saw their own experience reflected in the biblical accounts of "cities of refuge" found in Exodus 21:12–14, Numbers 35:9–34, Deuteronomy 19:1–13, and Joshua 20:1–9.

According to Mosaic law as described in the Bible, the Israelites were to create six cities of refuge where those who committed manslaughter could flee. In the honor-shame culture of biblical times, the relatives of a slain family member might retaliate even if the death was accidental or committed without malice aforethought. To allow for due process in the event of accidental killings, cities of refuge were created to allow for a proper trial before the congregation. If the death was ruled accidental, the person who committed manslaughter was allowed to live their life in the protection of the city of refuge for a time (until the death of the current high priest), to allow the bad blood to settle. Reflecting upon these biblical passages in light of their own situation as refugees, Central

American migrants developed their own "Brown Theology" of sanctuary. They understood that the right of due process for those falsely accused was a core spiritual principle underlying the creation of sanctuary cities in the Bible. It was important for those who accidentally killed another person without malice aforethought to be given a fair trial and for their lives to be protected by the community of believers. In the same way, it was a moral right of Central American migrants accused of "illegal immigration" to be given a fair hearing to determine whether or not they indeed qualified for asylum status according to U.S. and international law.

Because of the diplomatic politics of Central America and the U.S. war against communism, thousands of migrants were being denied due process for their asylum cases and deported back to perilous situations in Guatemala and El Salvador. In the same way that the biblical community of God was required to guarantee due process through the creation of cities of refuge, so should the churches of God in the United States serve as modern-day "sanctuaries" for refugees until they could receive due process in their asylum cases. This was the Brown Theology that undergirded the Sanctuary Movement of the 1980s, and it was developed by the migrants themselves, organic theologians who brought with them their ideas, formed by their experiences, and helped create a movement to welcome and protect "the stranger" in the United States.

The Sanctuary Movement in Los Angeles

Under the leadership of Claretian priest Luis Olivares, the Brown Church played a focal role in the development of the Sanctuary Movement in Los Angeles, central to the Sanctuary Movement because it served as a figurative Ellis Island for many migrants and also as a transfer station for many who were eventually directed to other cities in the United States and Canada (Chinchilla, Hamilton, and Loucky 2009, 109–110). Like Archbishop Oscar Romero, Father Luis had a "second conversion" to the poor and marginalized. In his case it was César Chávez, Dolores Huerta, and the farmworkers movement that reshaped his view of ministry and the Gospel. Olivares recounted, "I live a double standard as a cleric and I guess, as a Mexican American. One of the greatest things that has happened to me, as to my involvement with the United Farm Workers, is an awareness as to where life really is. The things that are of value to farmworkers give you a totally different perspective. You start seeing the dimensions of the gospel. [It has had] a tremendous influence on me" (quoted in García 2008, 217–218).

It was as parish priest of La Placita Church across from Olvera Street in downtown Los Angeles where Father Olivares would go on to help launch the Sanctuary Movement in the 1980s. This historic church's founding in 1781 marked the birth of the city, and in the 1980s it was flourishing with eleven Spanish-language masses that were attended by both Central American and Mexican immigrants. During that decade, Los Angeles grew as a center of Salvadoran migration and as a city with the second largest population of Salvadoreños outside of San Salvador.

As the number of Central American refugees and asylum seekers continued to increase in the La Placita congregation, Father Louie—as Olivares was affectionately known—together with Father Richard Estrada, Episcopalian leader Lydia Lopez, and Jesuit priest Michael Kennedy, pastor of Dolores Mission in East Los Angeles, developed a ministry of sanctuary and holistic support. On December 12, 1985, the feast day of La Virgen de Guadalupe, La Placita was declared the first Catholic sanctuary church in Los Angeles. The pronouncement was made as part of a large public gathering featuring eighty religious leaders of various faiths, celebrities from film and television, and, most importantly, the Central American refugee community (García 2008, 226). At the press conference that accompanied the event, Father Olivares proclaimed, "Today, December 12, 1985, on the feast day of Our Lady of Guadalupe, the patroness of the Americas, we here at La Placita Church in unity with our brothers and sisters of other faiths publicly declare the church to be a sanctuary for refugees fleeing persecution and oppression in Central America. These Salvadorans and Guatemaltecos are our brothers and sisters also and we will not turn them away" (García 2008, 226). Those in attendance further verbally covenanted to stand with the Central American community in their suffering as well as to advocate for the end of violence and war in their homelands. This verbal covenant was read aloud in the service:

Do we as a community of faith commit ourselves to support our brothers and sisters from Central America?

WE DO.

Do we commit ourselves to work together to end the violence, the war and the torture so prevalent in these countries?

WE DO.

Do we commit ourselves to work together to bring about peace with justice in all of Central America?

WE DO.

My brothers and sisters we have just publicly declared and committed ourselves here at our Lady Queen of Angeles Church to provide Sanctuary for Central American refugees. (García 2018, 331)

As a sanctuary congregation, La Placita each day offered shelter to as many as two hundred refugees and asylum seekers, who slept on and underneath church pews. Women and children were placed with Mexican American families and also at Blessed Sacrament Church in Hollywood. In addition to the provision of housing, Olivares, Lopez, and other pastoral staff offered food, transportation, clothing, English-language instruction, and legal assistance. Employment was also secured through the broader sanctuary network in Los Angeles, which included Jewish synagogues and mainline Protestant denominations. The Centro Pastoral Rutilio Grande, named after one of the first Salvadoran martyrs, was created to coordinate these various ministry efforts. Father Luis was also the first chairperson of the Coalition for Humane Immigrant Rights of Los Angeles (CHIRLA).

In addition to the laudable efforts of La Placita Church, it is important to note that the Central American community itself also created important humanitarian organizations in Los Angeles that partnered with both secular and religious activists. Two of these organizations were El Rescate, founded in 1981, and the Central American Resource Center (CARECEN), established in 1983 (Chinchilla, Hamilton, and Loucky 2009, 108). El Rescate and CARECEN supplied social services for asylees in the forms of legal representation, medical care, food provision, and English-language classes (Chinchilla, Hamilton, and Loucky 2009, 109, 118).

The legal advocacy efforts of the Sanctuary Movement came to important fruition in the *American Baptist Churches v. Thornburgh* Settlement Agreement (ABC Agreement, 1991) and the passage of the Nicaraguan Adjustment and Central American Relief Act (NACARA, 1997). The ABC Agreement represented the culmination of a five-year federal lawsuit filed by a coalition of religious groups including the American Baptist denomination, together with human rights organizations such as the National Lawyers Guild and the American Civil Liberties Union. Plaintiffs asserted that migrants from Guatemala and El Salvador had been denied due process in their asylum petitions. As evidence, they showed that in 1984 less than 1 percent of applicants from Guatemala and 3 percent from El Salvador were granted asylum. As part of the settlement agreement, the U.S. government agreed to review de novo the asylum cases of hundreds of thousands of refugees from El Salvador and Guatemala. In addition, these asylum seekers were granted TPS from deportation and work permits as they waited for their cases to be processed. The Immigration Act of 1990 further solidified the legal gains of the ABC Agreement. This law granted TPS to Salvadorans, and upon the expiration of TPS in 1992, Salvadorans became eligible for a new Deferred Enforced Departure program as well as asylum under the terms of the ABC Agreement (Barba and Castillo-Ramos 2019, 19–20).

Faced with an overwhelming backlog of asylum cases from Central America, Congress, in 1997, passed the Nicaraguan Adjustment and Central American Relief Act. This legislation granted legal permanent residency to hundreds of thousands of registered asylum seekers who had resided in the United States since at least December 1, 1990. Together, *American Baptist Churches v. Thornburgh* and NACARA transformed the lives of hundreds of thousands of Central American refugees and represent two of the most important civil rights victories in modern times. The Sanctuary Movement was central to these victories.

The New Sanctuary Movement, 2006–2010

In addition to NACARA and TPS, the passage of the Immigration Reform and Control Act in 1986 ushered in further relief insofar as it normalized the legal statuses of 2.7 million undocumented immigrants from Latin America, Asia, and other parts of the globe. In the ensuing years, however, the U.S. economy increased its dependency upon the inexpensive labor of millions of undocumented immigrants. As a result, in order to fill the United States' ravenous need for cheap labor, approximately 850,000 undocumented immigrants came to the United States on an annual basis from 2000 to 2005, and by 2006 the number of unauthorized immigrants from Latin America, Asia, Africa, and Europe had swelled to 11.6 million (Hoefer, Rytina, and Campbell 2006).

The U.S. government largely turned a blind eye to undocumented immigration during these years because of the massive economic contributions such immigrants made to the GDP and federal tax rolls. In 2006, for example, unauthorized immigrants contributed $428 billion to the nation's $13.6 trillion GDP (Romero 2016, 28). According to Stephen C. Goss, the chief actuary of the Social Security Administration, moreover, unauthorized immigrants contributed up to $240 billion to the Social Security trust fund by 2007, even though they are not eligible to receive Social Security payments (Romero 2016, 29). If not for these monumental tax contributions from undocumented immigrants with false Social Security numbers, the Social Security Administration would have experienced payment shortfalls as early as 2009 (Romero 2016, 29).

Yet by the mid-2000s, widescale immigration from Mexico and other parts of Latin America engendered a rabid anti-immigrant backlash, most notably through the conservative populist Tea Party movement. The passage of the Sensenbrenner Bill, formally the Border Protection, Anti-terrorism, and Illegal Immigration Control Act, by the House of Representatives in December 2005 was the most virulent legislative expression of such xenophobia. This bill, which never passed the Senate, sought to construct a seven-hundred-mile-long fence along the U.S.-Mexico border, eliminate the Diversity Immigrant Visa Program, categorize all forms of unlawful presence and visa overstays as felonies, and criminalize churches that ministered to undocumented immigrants (Romero 2016, 20; Yukich 2013, 5). In addition, it called for harsher sentences for immigrant documentation fraud and increased penalties for those who knowingly hired undocumented workers (Barba and Castillo-Ramos 2019). In response to the Sensenbrenner Bill, an estimated 3.5 to 5.1 million Latinas/os took to the streets in protest in more than 160 cities across the United States (Barreto et al. 2009). Out of these protests, the New Sanctuary Movement was born. On May 9, 2007, religious advocates from Chicago, Los Angeles, New York, San Diego, and Seattle held joint press conferences to announce the launch of a national interfaith network that they termed the New Sanctuary Movement (NSM) (Yukich 2013, 5).

CLUE, based in Los Angeles and led by Alexia Salvatierra, Interfaith Worker Justice (IWJ), housed in Chicago, and Father Juan Carlos Ruiz, a Catholic priest in New York City, served as midwives for the NSM (Yukich 2013, 35). Both CLUE and IWJ possessed extensive membership networks, leadership infrastructures, and financial resources that made the establishment of the NSM possible. Undocumented immigrant leader Elvira Arellano, together with her organization, La Familia Latina Unida (LFLU), and Methodist pastors Walter Coleman and Emma Lozano also played important leadership roles in the movement (Yukich 2013, 35; Hondagneu-Sotelo 2008, 149). Arellano became the public face of the NSM after claiming sanctuary in the Adalberto United Methodist Church of Chicago (Yukich 2013, 35; Hondagneu-Sotelo 2008, 149). Unlike the original Sanctuary Movement, which focused on the provision of literal sanctuary in churches as well as policy relief, for thousands of recently arrived asylum seekers the main goal of the NSM was the passage of comprehensive immigration reform for immigrant families who had already lived in the United States for many years.

Sociologist Grace Yukich further argues that the NSM was a paradigmatic example of a *multi-target social movement*, "a movement or movement organization that simultaneously seeks to change multiple institutions—in this case [NSM], both religious and governmental institutions" (Yukich 2013, 3). As a multi-target social movement, the NSM sought both to challenge unjust U.S. immigration policy as well as to stir the hearts and minds of religious communities toward compassion for the immigrant community. In the words of Yukich, "They fought to create 'one family under God': to keep immigrant families united and to change the hearts and minds of religious people, turning them toward a religious worldview that embraces all people as members of one divine and human family" (9). A further goal of the NSM was to disabuse the wider U.S. public of the notion that Christianity was synonymous with xenophobic social conservatism (Yukich 2013, 8–9).

In the following narrative, Alexia Salvatierra, who served as executive director of CLUE, gives her firsthand account of the founding and development of the NSM. Though some scholarly accounts of the NSM have been published, Salvatierra's oral history represents the first such written account by a movement leader. Her testimony offers a unique analysis of the origins, methods, and policy goals of the NSM as well as the reasons for the eventual failure of comprehensive immigration reform. Salvatierra also supplies one of the first accounts of evangelical community organizing efforts during this time period as part of the Evangelical Immigration Table.

The New Sanctuary Movement: A Firsthand Account

Alexia Salvatierra describes her experiences of the movement she cofounded in the following paragraphs.

In December 2005, the Sensenbrenner Bill passed the House of Representatives. A draconian response to immigration, it would have made it a felony to be undocumented or to help or serve an undocumented individual. This sent shock waves through the majority of the ten million plus undocumented residents of the United States who had been here for over a decade. Terror, confusion, grief, rage—these reactions moved through the Latina/o community. The faith communities and institutions where these individuals and families belonged were similarly affected. On Ash Wednesday of 2006, Cardinal Roger Mahony of the Archdiocese of Los Angeles preached a sermon saying that if Sensenbrenner were to pass the Senate, he would call on every Catholic across the country to continue to serve people regardless of their immigration status even if they were to go to prison as a result. His action inspired former Sanctuary Movement members to begin conversations all over the country about whether it was time for a new Sanctuary Movement. Walter "Slim" Coleman and his wife Emma Lozano were pastoring Adalberto United Methodist Church in Chicago when their parishioner, Elvira, received a final deportation order. She moved into the church building, and they declared their church a sanctuary.

Groups meeting in Los Angeles and New York were inspired by Elvira's case, but it is also clear that the situation in 2006 was significantly different than it had been in 1980. First, the public policy goals of sanctuary in the eighties were simple, clear, and realistic—to change the asylum system to provide equal protection to individuals fleeing U.S.

allies, create a mechanism for Central Americans to receive protection as a group, and stop the funding to governments in Central America that enabled the civil wars to continue. The public policy goals of the movement in 2006 were much more ambitious and complex, including passing comprehensive immigration reform and ending forced deportations of undocumented immigrants. Secondly, the asylum seekers who were arriving in the eighties needed shelter in churches or in the homes of church members; they had little to no possessions and knew nothing about how to survive in the United States. In 2006, the vast majority of people facing deportation had no need or desire to live in a house of worship or even with another family. They were established with their own homes, jobs, and communities. Many were active members or leaders of primarily immigrant congregations. They merely wanted to be safe from deportation. Third, in the eighties a case could easily be made that deportation meant death. In 2006, deportation would more likely mean uprooting a family or separating citizen children from their immigrant parents, taking away employees and neighbors who were part of the essential fabric of their churches and communities—a very different case.

Juan Carlos Ruiz, a priest in New York, and I were both part of these conversations in our respective cities. We met at the Mexican American Cultural Center in San Antonio in October 2006 and came up with an alternative idea. We would seek families with a final order of deportation and a revealing case (a case that demonstrated the injustice of the existing immigration system) who were willing, out of their own faith and activist commitment, to make the sacrifice and take the risk to live in churches and publicize their stories. We would mount an extensive publicity campaign. The goal would be to change public opinion and support the passage of comprehensive immigration reform. In 2007, polls showed that a large percentage of U.S. residents supported the McCain-Kennedy Comprehensive Immigration Reform Act, including 78 percent who responded that undocumented immigrants should be given a chance at citizenship (Soerens and Hwang 2009). There was a high degree of support for McCain-Kennedy among Catholic, Jewish, and Muslim religious leaders, but evangelical leaders were divided (Cooperman 2006). By the time that we called a meeting of friends and colleagues in both cities to discuss the idea in the first week of 2007, representatives from coalitions in thirty-seven cities were on the call. We believed that the Holy Spirit clearly was moving.

From January to June 2007, we received over four thousand media hits, including an episode of a television drama show focused on the movement and a front-page story in *Time* magazine. The courageous families who went into sanctuary and became the spokespeople for the movement went through a barrage of negative reactions and personal harassment. The Minutemen, an anti-immigrant vigilante group from the border region, stood outside of sanctuary churches on Sunday mornings and disrupted services by yelling obscenities and threats.

The responses of the churches varied, but one particular response went viral and became a paradigmatic symbol of the impact of the movement. Lutheran pastor Cesar Arroyo was a Peruvian immigrant whose primarily immigrant congregation in the San Fernando Valley of Los Angeles provided physical sanctuary for a Guatemalan asylum seeker. He saw on the internet that the Minutemen were coming to harass his church on Easter Sunday. He told his congregation that they did not need to show up that Sunday; he did not want to subject his undocumented members to abuse or trauma. Leaders from other churches planned to attend in solidarity, including the local Catholic priest and Lutheran bishop Dean Nelson. Without Arroyo's knowledge, his church leaders developed a different plan. The whole congregation showed up on Sunday; between the visitors and the members, the church was packed to the rafters. The Minutemen did show up and carried out their plan. However, after the church service, the members led a procession around the outside of the church, with Lutheran bishop Nelson in the front row, singing hymns. They then stopped in front of the shouting group of Minutemen and began to pray for them. The Minutemen slowly fell silent. One member of the Minutemen group who was filming on his camera mused out loud about their purpose: "What kind of trick is this? What are they trying to accomplish?" After they were finished praying, they processed back into the church. Pastor Arroyo and the local Catholic priest were last. Pastor Arroyo turned to the Minutemen and said, "God bless America." Several of them responded, "God bless America." A local Univision reporter said to Pastor Arroyo, "I have never seen anything like this in twenty years of covering immigration. You may make me a Christian." The Minutemen never returned; however, Pastor Arroyo's petition to the federal immigration agency to bring his son from Peru was "lost" multiple times.

Some of the immigrant leaders who were the spokespeople of the movement were able to resolve their cases; others were able to attain deferred deportation and safely return home. Still others left with their cases unresolved or lost and slid back into the shadows where undocumented people live. Elvira left Adalberto United Methodist publicly and was deported after a press conference in Los Angeles. The bipartisan proposal for immigration reform (sponsored by Ted Kennedy and John McCain, two Irish Americans from immigrant ancestry on different sides of the political aisle) that went before the Senate for a vote in June 2007 did not succeed.

Ali Noorani, a young, secular Muslim who was leading the largest moderate organization working on immigration reform, the National Immigration Forum, arrived at an analysis of the loss. The coalition supporting immigration reform was too narrow; they needed to bring in a greater number of moderate voices. Top leadership at World Relief, the relief and development organization of the National Association of Evangelicals, agreed. World Relief leaders Matt Soerens and Jenny Yang had already partnered with Willow Creek, one of the largest evangelical megachurches in the country, on congregational education around immigration. Their experience showed them that there was in fact a door opening to move the evangelical church.

At the same time in Southern California, I was coming to a parallel but different conclusion. I saw the narrowness of the movement as a result of the lack of passion on the part of nonimmigrants and the lack of hope on the part of immigrants. While polls consistently showed that a strong majority of American citizens supported the basic tenets of comprehensive immigration reform—toward a system that would be more effective, logical, just, and humane, they did not prioritize the issue. It did not affect them personally. The majority of citizens who felt passionately about the issue were against a more open and generous immigration system—seeing immigrants as economic or cultural threats. While this group was in the minority, their passion provoked them to greater ongoing engagement (Matos 2021). Mario Lopez, director of the Republican Congressional Hispanic Conference at that time, reported that the ratio of phone calls to Congress was overwhelmingly against the immigration bill: "I would say it runs about 10 to one, and there are days when it can be 20, 25 to one" (quoted in Ludden 2007).

Most immigrants and their citizen family members, on the other hand, had great passion about the issue but did not participate in advocacy activities. Groups like Esperanza USA (a network of fifteen thousand Latina/o churches) and the NHCLC (National Hispanic Christian Leadership Council) organized within the Latina/o evangelical community but were not integrated into broader immigration organizing efforts, nor were they able to engage the majority of Latina/o Christian leaders. I saw that by bringing immigrant and nonimmigrant evangelicals together in equal partnerships of intimate solidarity that we could achieve an exchange of hope and passion, expanding and strengthening advocacy efforts in both communities. I was the executive director at the time of CLUE-CA, a statewide interfaith economic justice ministry that had been the lead organization for the New Sanctuary Movement.

We had a chapter in Orange County, a national bastion for the evangelical movement, home of multiple megachurches and Vanguard University and Biola University in nearby southeast Los Angeles County. Wendy Tarr and Vanessa Martinez staffed the Orange County work. Both were leaders in their respective evangelical communities. Together, they organized a pastors' breakfast on immigration that brought together twenty-six white evangelical pastors, twenty-six Latina/o evangelical pastors, and one Korean American megachurch pastor. At the breakfast, the attendees discussed immigration as a pastoral issue; Latina/o pastors shared their anguish about the impact of the current system on their congregations—the dreams broken and families separated by deportation. The white pastors shared their fear of losing members if they got involved. Dr. Juan Martinez, academic dean of the Centro Latino at Fuller Theological Seminary at the time, challenged the assembly to move beyond fear. He asked, "Are we not the people who are called to carry the Cross?" His words moved the group into an honest discussion about what would be required to bring their congregations along. They decided to start the Our Children / Nuestros Hijos project, which would train and engage members of predominantly white and predominantly Latina/o congregations to minister together to unaccompanied children in a local detention center in Fullerton. The trust relationships formed between volunteers then would create encounters where the exchange of passion and hope would occur. These volunteers would then become seeds of change in their respective congregations.

The Our Children / Nuestros Hijos project served its multiple purposes. Vacation Bible school, baking classes, and soccer brought immigrant and nonimmigrant volunteers into a partnership that changed hearts and minds. A major leader at Mariners Church (an eighteen-thousand-member primarily white megachurch in Newport Beach) walked into the office of the senior pastor and urged him to bring the issue before the church board and initiate a study group, using Matt Soerens and Jenny Hwang's book *Welcoming the Stranger*. These efforts resulted in the organization of the Loving the Stranger Coalition, which at one point boasted as members thirteen megachurches, including two megachurches of color. When the coalition visited one prominent conservative legislator, he had prepared all his anti-immigration credentials for them and was in shock when they advocated for comprehensive immigration reform.

A parallel CLUE-CA project in South Los Angeles bringing together predominantly African American churches and predominantly Latina/o immigrant churches succeeded similarly. At a meeting in Washington, D.C., in October 2010, Jenny Yang, Galen Carey (public policy staff for the National Association of Evangelicals), and I discussed the possibility of uniting our efforts, bringing in other allies in the evangelical community and including the major Latina/o evangelical networks. That discussion led to the first meeting of the Evangelical Immigration Table (EIT) at the offices of the progressive evangelical nonprofit Sojourners in Washington, D.C., on February 28, 2011. World Relief had allocated Jenny Yang's time up to the end of February to try to build this broader coalition. On February 28, the last day of the month, all the travel schedules of some of the most prominent evangelical leaders in the nation coincided and the EIT was born.

On June 12, 2012, the EIT held its first public press conference in the Rayburn Room of the Capitol, with the broadest representation of evangelical leaders and signatories standing for a justice cause since the movement to abolish slavery. Members of Focus on the Family, Southern Baptist Leadership, Sojourners, World Relief and World Vision, the National Association of Evangelicals, NALEC (a coalition of younger and more progressive Latina/o evangelical leaders), NHCLC, Esperanza USA, Intervarsity Christian Fellowship, and Navigators all stood up and signed on to the EIT. On June 14, President Obama issued the executive order to implement DACA—Deferred Action for Childhood Arrivals. In a private phone call to an EIT leader, the president expressed gratitude for EIT, saying that it would have been much harder to issue the order if not for their public support.

The EIT led to the formation of Bibles, Business, and Badges, a broader coalition of moderates and conservatives for comprehensive immigration reform, under the umbrella of Ali Noorani's organization, the National Immigration Forum. The work of these coalitions was instrumental to the passage of a bipartisan immigration bill by the Senate in 2013. However, the bill stalled in the House, where it was not brought to the floor for a vote. (Advocates had estimated that there would have been sufficient bipartisan support to pass the bill in the House as well if it had come to a vote.)

At the same time that the EIT was doing its work, other efforts in the faith community also intensified. Although the NSM lost its lead agency (CLUE) and became a loose network of individual coalitions, members continued to protect and defend immigrants facing potential deportation. They also shifted their advocacy efforts to focus on an achievable regulatory policy goal—prosecutorial discretion and a robust deferred deportation program for undocumented immigrants who had not been convicted of criminal activity and had a record of economic and community contributions. Because the prioritization of immigration enforcement on convicted felons was a key element of the Obama immigration program, instituted through the Morton Memo in August 2010, this goal was feasible. In the memo, ICE director John Morton instructed all ICE employees to focus the agency's limited resources on individuals who posed a serious threat to public safety or national security (ICE 2010).

The Interfaith Immigration Coalition (engaging most of the mainline Protestant denominations and the Hebrew Immigrant Aid Society—HIAS—the oldest Jewish immigration organization) and Justice for Immigrants (the Roman Catholic internal organization working on immigration issues) continued to advocate for the DREAM Act, comprehensive immigration reform, and related pro-immigrant policies. Thus, the NSM, like its 1980s predecessor, played an important role in achieving significant changes to immigration policy. Still, the dream of comprehensive immigration reform was again deferred.

The Centrality of Faith

The history detailed in this chapter clearly shows the centrality of faith-based organizations and leaders in U.S. movements advocating for immigrants over the past century. And contrary to some scholarship and public perceptions, the leaders of many of these faith-based movements were primarily immigrants themselves, particularly those of Latina/o ancestry. Indeed, the faith-based movements that have been the most powerful for immigrant rights have been led or co-led by immigrants. The most effective movements have also used the sanctuary strategy of combining efforts to house, accompany, and care for individual vulnerable immigrants with strong grassroots public policy advocacy.

This history also shows the potential, as well as the difficulties, of uniting broad coalitions of religious believers of different races/ethnicities and theological perspectives into a single movement. In addition, it illuminates along with Yukich (2013) that the multiple goals of a multi-target social movement like the Sanctuary Movement often conflict with each other, as strategies to achieve one goal sometimes complicate the strategies of another goal.

In the following chapters we turn to the more recent history of the Trump administration's aggressive enforcement policies and how they spurred a new iteration of the faith-based movement to defend, accompany, and advocate for vulnerable immigrants.

2

Context

While the New Sanctuary Movement continued without a lead agency from 2008 to 2013, it received less public attention and experienced diminished participation. Church World Service took responsibility for supporting the movement in 2013, at a moment when yet another bipartisan comprehensive immigration bill failed. While this bill had flaws, it also contained sound, sensible, and sane policy initiatives that would have alleviated human suffering, strengthened families, and benefited the United States and immigrants' countries of origin economically. The wave of support arising through widespread organizing, including major efforts on the part of faith communities, almost carried the bill to victory. The reason for the bill's defeat revealed the core issue that the struggle for immigration reform has faced since that date. While there were enough Democratic and Republican votes to pass the bill, it was derailed by a handful of congressional representatives who saw it as a political advantage for the problem to remain unsolved and a political disadvantage to be seen as welcoming to immigrants.

The perspective of these legislators was prescient; Donald Trump went on to make the presumed threat posed by immigrants and the need for intensified border enforcement a signature issue of his campaign and presidency. As one of his first post-inaugural acts as president, Trump signed an executive order on January 25, 2017, eliminating the directives established under the Obama administration that prioritized for removal only those noncitizens who had criminal convictions. This order directed ICE to enforce U.S. laws against "all removable aliens" (Executive Order 13768, 2017). This order also directed DHS to hire an additional ten thousand ICE officers to increase enforcement. As a result of this policy, the percentage of immigrants arrested by ICE who had no criminal record more than doubled over the course of the Trump administration (Pierce and Bolter 2020) and the number of people detained by ICE over the course of a year reached a record high in 2019 at more than 510,000 (DHS 2019a), including over 69,000 children (Sherman, Mendoza, and Burke 2019). The rhetoric and actions of the Trump presidency energized the faith community in response.

Immediately after the election in November 2016, a group of sixty faith-based organizers from around the country called an emergency in-person meeting at the historic Highlander Center in Tennessee to pray, lament, and strategize. Alexia Salvatierra, in attendance, describes this meeting:

> After Donald Trump's victory in 2016, faith leaders and organizers throughout the nation knew that the vulnerable people we worked with were likely to be in danger. Sixty of us came together to pray and discern what God wanted us to do. We ended up breaking up into small groups focused on different areas of concern. The immigration group was deeply worried, knowing the role that immigration had played in the campaign. We decided that the limitation of earlier faith-based efforts was that they were too leader-focused. Clergy and congregational leadership had become advocates—but most members of congregations knew little to nothing about the issue and took their perspective from their media of choice. We felt that we needed to go deeper, to get members of local congregations to create a heart-based connection with the people who would be most affected by the potential restrictions and rights violations that were projected. We wanted to see immigrant and nonimmigrant congregations working together in this process to create the exchange of hope and passion and to ensure that nonimmigrants were not coming from a charity perspective. By the time the conversation was done (a conversation that both Dr. Robert Chao Romero and I participated in), we had a vision of bringing people of faith together across the dividing lines to protect and defend vulnerable immigrant families facing deportation. We chose Matthew 25 for Jesus's statement about his identification with migrants.

In addition to the emergence of the Matthew 25 / Mateo 25 organization described by Dr. Salvatierra, Church World Service's assumption of the lead agency role, under the leadership of Rev. Noel Anderson, provided an important shot in the arm to the New Sanctuary Movement at this key moment. Strong sanctuary coalitions continued in eighteen cities across the United States, increasingly occupying a particular niche within the broader immigrant rights movement. As the mixed record of the Obama administration transferred over to an unprecedented level of attack on immigrants and the immigration system during the Trump administration, sanctuary became a vehicle for progressive congregations horrified by the inhumanity of the Trump regulatory policy to take a dramatic stand in solidarity. Sanctuary congregations also became a refuge of last resort for certain families with final deportation orders. Without the option of deferred deportation, mixed-status families across the country moved into buildings owned by religious entities, while other congregations contributed financial support and participation in public policy advocacy actions. By the end of the Trump administration, roughly eleven hundred congregations were listed in the sanctuary database as engaged with the movement in some form. A broader circle participated in "sanctuary in the streets," activities online or in person that expressed solidarity with immigrants. The faith-based sanctuary network focused intensive energy on supporting the municipal Sanctuary Movement—the push for municipalities, counties, and states to refuse to turn over information about immigrants in their localities to federal law enforcement under most conditions.

During the Trump administration, the broader faith-based movement for immigrant justice found common cause in issues beyond sanctuary. Trump's zero-tolerance policy, which resulted in the separation of children from their parents at the border in 2017, provoked such broad opposition, including from a wide range of faith communities, that the administration actually dropped the policy—one of the few instances in which Trump's administration actually stepped back from a move to discourage or restrict immigration. The administration's drastic lowering of the caps on refugee resettlement (pre-COVID-19) from an average of sixty thousand to eighteen thousand per year also provoked broad religious reaction. In the latter case, strong reactions by faith leaders, including moderate and conservative faith leaders, did not have any appreciable effect on administration policies.

During the Trump administration, denominational and regional initiatives to protect, defend, and support immigrants harmed by draconian policies were also begun and strengthened.

Faith-Based Immigrant Justice in Context

To understand the impact of faith-based movements for immigrant justice, it is critically important to place them in context—with respect to both the other kinds of immigrant ministry practiced by faith communities and their role in the major broad-based secular movements for immigrant justice.

Most Christian denominations have ethnic-specific ministries, some of which serve communities in which the majority are immigrants or relatives of immigrants. (Non-Christian religious traditions, communities, and institutions also serve large numbers of immigrants but often without a specific ethnic focus.) Many Christian denominations and religious organizations also have peace and justice ministries that include immigration as an issue area. The interaction between ethnic-specific ministries and ministries that seek justice for immigrants is complex and varied. The majority of ethnic-specific ministries serve and engage both immigrants and nonimmigrants. However, neither nonimmigrants nor immigrants in these communities automatically share a common vision about the kind of immigration system that they would favor or support.

Immigrants in general do not always support liberal immigration policy, for a wide variety of reasons (Krogstad and Lopez 2021). Immigrants with more conservative theological positions that emphasize hierarchy and boundaries tend to respect the rule of law as it currently exists as part of their commitment to obedience to God (understanding suffering for the sake of obedience as purifying). Immigrant Protestant congregations tend to be strongly evangelical and often charismatic. This can create natural alliances with conservative white Pentecostals and evangelicals who share their theological views and spiritual experiences. Immigrant evangelicals (and Catholic charismatics) are grateful to their nonimmigrant coreligionists and tend to support their positions on political issues out of respect and loyalty (even when it creates emotional and cognitive dissonance). Paradoxically, it is common in Latina/o congregations to pray for relatives to cross the border safely even as leaders and members feel shame for and with those who have broken the law.

Even if immigrants in these congregations do support advocating for an effective and humane immigration system, their priority may be their individual or family advancement rather than political action. They may focus their service activities on enabling their members and neighbors to survive and to get ahead in spite of the current restrictions. The struggle for the improvement of immigration policy may be perceived as draining time, energy, and resources for an unlikely goal. When progressive white Christians who are often the leaders of national denominational peace and justice ministries push immigrant congregations to engage in advocacy, there can be a mixture of suspicion about their broader theological and political perspectives and resentment about yet again having white people think that they know more about their needs than they do. Yet when it occurs, as we saw in the last chapter, the leadership of immigrants themselves in struggles for immigrant justice can provide the most powerful inspiration and leadership for broader engagement.

There are also other faith-based national organizations that include immigration in their list of issues. Sojourners, the long-standing progressive evangelical magazine and advocacy organization, has a department working on immigration advocacy. Organizations such as Christians for Social Action, Red Letter Christians, Evangelicals 4 Social Justice, and Freedom Road include immigration advocacy in their issue list. Hispanic-serving organizations such as the National Hispanic Christian Leadership Council (NHCLC) and the National Latino Evangelical Coalition (NALEC) include immigrant rights and immigration reform in their objectives.

Broad-Based Movements for Immigrant Justice

Social movement theory is a robust and diverse field with fierce arguments; the general consensus, however, is that activity toward social change becomes a movement when the participants go beyond those who are directly affected to include the spontaneous participation of a broader public (Goodwin and Jasper 2014). Millions of people, the majority of whom had never previously been involved in an immigrant rights organization, came out to protest the Sensenbrenner Bill on May 1, 2006. The spines of movements, however, are organizations and networks of organizations. For movements to go beyond a few isolated actions into a long-term, effective campaign, organizations must follow up with spontaneous participants and engage them in the ongoing work, intentionally increasing their commitment and capacity over time (Goodwin and Jasper 2014).

The organizations that carry on the ongoing work toward immigrant justice in the United States fit into two basic categories—those led by immigrants that focus on organizing immigrants and those led by allies and immigrants in collaboration that focus on organizing the general public. Within these categories is a continuum between moderate and progressive leaders, subgroups, and organizations. This difference between moderate and progressive can be simply defined as the willingness to compromise in the understanding that small gains over time can turn into major change, versus holding out for more substantial change even though it may not be achievable in the near future. Struggles between these factions have weakened the power and impact of the movement at key moments.

While organizations advocating for immigrant rights come and go (often hiring the same people in new configurations), there is a relatively short list of major players who continue to work diligently on the issue on a national level. These include networks of local and regional organizations that come together with a broader social justice agenda, such as Community Change's FIRM (Fair Immigration Reform Movement), which includes local organizations in thirty states, and the major national community organizing networks (Faith in Action and Gamaliel, which both specifically include immigration in their broader program). There are also organizations with another central purpose for whom immigration is an important side issue—such as progressive labor unions (the Change to Win Federation, which is led by the Service Employees International Union and UNITE HERE) and research think tanks such as the Hope Border Institute.[1] Other organizations focus solely on immigrants and immigration—either as legal service providers with an organizing arm or as nonprofits focused on immigrant organizing and/or policy change (which might also provide legal assistance as an ongoing service). This latter group of organizations includes Central American Resource Center (CARECEN), the oldest and largest network of Central American–led legal, service, and advocacy organizations, and Al Otro Lado (a legal service organization that works with asylum seekers on both sides of the Mexico-U.S. border). There are also groups that serve and organize a specific constituency: United We Dream focuses on young people brought to the United States as minors. NAKASEC (National Korean American Service and Education Consortium), the Asian American Pacific Islander Table, and Asian Americans Advancing Justice are some of the strongest associations focused on advocating for Asian and Pacific Islander immigrants. BAJI (Black Alliance for Just Immigration) organizes and focuses on African immigrants. Last, Movimiento Cosecha is a new group led primarily by young immigrants with an organizing focus on civil rights for immigrants.

In general, the national organizations contribute information on national legislative developments and timely opportunities for positive change. They also offer various educational resources, including access to research studies. When possible and relevant, local groups will link their actions with national actions. Faith leaders often create a particular faith-based contribution to a broad-based action coordinated by these groups. In the section below we focus on some of the national organizations that work regularly with faith-based groups, including the cases featured in this book.

The National Immigration Forum

Since 1982, the National Immigration Forum has been a major leader in the arena of moderate immigration public policy advocacy. The phrase used in their mission statement is "responsible federal immigration policies, addressing today's economic and national security needs while honoring the ideals of our Founding Fathers, who created America as a land of opportunity" (National Immigration Forum n.d.). The forum is the umbrella organization for the Evangelical Immigration Table (EIT). It is also a major partner for Matthew 25 / Mateo 25. Ali Noorani, the president and chief executive officer, is a secular Muslim with deep roots in immigrant communities and with a commitment to enabling the United States to live up to its stated ideals. The National Immigration Forum understands the actual and potential roles played by moderate and conservative faith leaders in educating and mobilizing these sectors of society.

National Day Laborers Organizing Network (NDLON)

Formally established in 2001, NDLON involves over fifty grassroots day laborer organizations across the United States. Given that the majority of day laborers are undocumented immigrants, immigration has always been one of its core foci. NDLON's immigration work rises out of the daily life experiences of its members and seeks to provide a vehicle for their voices and goals. As such, NDLON is more concerned about faithfully pursuing its members' goals than discerning whether a particular policy goal is realistic in the short term. As most NDLON members are people of faith, the group is hospitable to the participation and support of faith leaders, particularly immigrant faith leaders. The faith allies of NDLON tend to be politically progressive. NDLON works closely with CLUE, one of the organizations discussed at length later in this book. Its founder and co–executive director, Pablo Alvarado, is an immigrant from Central America who has worked as a day laborer and who, having been a base community organizer in El Salvador influenced by Archbishop Oscar Romero, appreciates the historic role of progressive faith leaders in Central America and the United States.

Coalition for Humane Immigration Reform (CHIRLA)

CHIRLA was founded in 1986 in Los Angeles by Father Luis Olivares, a leading voice in the original Sanctuary Movement. The group focuses on organizing immigrants to advance the human and civil rights of immigrants and refugees, including changes in public policy at multiple levels. CHIRLA occupies a middle position between NDLON and the National Immigration Forum, seeking both to be faithful to its core constituency and to be realistic about achievable policy goals in the short term. Executive director Angelica Salas is part of the group currently advising the Biden administration on immigration policy. CHIRLA is an active member of FIRM (the immigration network of Community Change). Although CHIRLA is a secular organization, its faith-based roots have continued to inform its work, creating an ongoing openness to collaboration with faith leaders and institutions. We Care, Matthew 25 / Mateo 25, LA Voice, and CLUE all work closely with CHIRLA, which regularly organizes broad coalition campaigns and actions across Southern California.

These local organizations also have organic relationships with national organizations. The United Methodists Welcoming Congregations Network partners with the national United Methodist Church, receiving resources and maintaining ongoing communication. They also work with the Interfaith Immigration Coalition, in which the United Methodist Church acts as a leader. The local Faith in Action chapters, such as LA Voice, work with the national Faith in Action organization. The Catholic Archdiocese of Los Angeles naturally works with the national Justice for Immigrants organization under the national Catholic Council of Bishops. Matthew 25 / Mateo 25, in its Diplomado training program for Latina/o pastoral leaders, works in partnership with Fuller Theological Seminary and with Sojourners.

Facing the Trump administration's wholesale attack on immigrant communities, these organizations worked together closely across their differences—but even working jointly, they were able to achieve very little at the federal policy level. No federal immigration legislation was passed during the Trump administration, although over four hundred regulatory changes were instituted through executive orders or internal instructions, all of which were restrictive in nature. The only national grassroots victories over the restrictive policies of the administration were the stopping of the widespread separation of parents from their children in 2017 and the release of some vulnerable detainees from immigration detention centers in the early days of the COVID-19 pandemic. These victories were due to widespread, broad, and persistent outcry through a wide variety of communication vehicles. In California, the victories of different levels and forms of "sanctuary" legislation (policies separating immigration enforcement from local law enforcement) resulted from broad collaboration across organizations.

The Role and Contribution of Faith: A Firsthand Account

How do faith-based efforts relate to the broader organizations and movement? What is their unique contribution? How do sanctuary movements fit into this bigger picture? Two firsthand accounts from Alexia Salvatierra illustrate this role and contribution:

In March 2006, the Judiciary Committee of the Senate was set to consider the Sensenbrenner Bill—the Border Protection, Anti-terrorism, and Illegal Immigration Control Act—coming from the House of Representatives. Angelica Salas, executive director of CHIRLA, called me, the director of CLUE-LA at the time, at six o'clock in the morning to ask if we could identify clergy who would be willing to go to Washington, D.C., to utilize their moral authority to inspire the Judiciary Committee to include ethical concerns in their deliberations. With the help of a volunteer who had worked as a travel agent, we were able to get thirty-seven clergy of all denominations, including the president of the Board of Rabbis of Northern California and veteran civil rights leader Rev. James M. Lawson Jr., to Washington. They entered the room where the Judiciary Committee was debating the issue and stood against all the walls visibly praying. Senator Dianne Feinstein began to talk about the Torah and her own ethical commitments as a Jew; the committee ended up including the moral questions around the legislation in their conversation. The restrictive Sensenbrenner law did not emerge from the committee and was not passed into legislation.

Another example of the power of faith to affect legislation was the nationwide campaign to protect dreamers—people who came to the United States as children without documents. On June 12, 2012, the Evangelical Immigration Table held its debut press conference in the Rayburn Room of the Capitol. The leaders who spoke on behalf of dreamers included those from the National Association of Evangelicals, both World Relief and World Vision, the national leadership of the Southern Baptists, Sojourners, the Christian Community Development Association, and Focus on the Family. Many others signed the initial statement of biblical principles that support a humane, just, and effective immigration system, including Intervarsity Christian Fellowship and the Navigators—two of the largest evangelical University Campus Ministry networks. On June 13, dreamers carried out sit-ins at multiple congressional offices. On December 14, President Obama proclaimed the executive order on Deferred Action for Childhood Arrivals. He then called EIT leaders and shared that he could not have done it without their bipartisan support. These stories recounted by Dr. Salvatierra illustrate the various gifts that faith communities in general bring to broader movements.

Mobilizing Faith and Moral Commitment

While everyone can be motivated by simple self-interest, people of sincere faith and moral integrity can also be inspired to courageous action and sacrificial love by authentically and effectively appealing to their faith. Countless individuals throughout the ages have suffered and died for their deepest convictions. The art and science of motivating people on the basis of their faith requires more than superficial understanding of the tenets of a particular religious tradition—preaching at people famously causes guilt and resentment without transformation. On the other hand, comprehending the heart of another's intimate spiritual struggles and becoming the ally of the part of them that wants to be their best can be enormously effective in motivating action even in the face of risk and danger. The EIT has used the "I Was a Stranger" pledge in their effort to change the hearts and minds of Christian legislators. The pledge uses a bookmark with forty scriptures relevant to the issue of immigration and challenges pastors, congregation members, and believers who are public decision makers to read one per day as part of their daily devotions, asking for discernment about God's call.

The biblical prophets also used symbols and rituals to communicate to the nonrational right hemisphere of the brain, which can be powerful not only for people who directly espouse a religious faith but also for those who may not be religious but hear the music—who believe a moral framework and/or are formed by a spiritual tradition that resonates with these images and experiences. When Martin Luther King Jr. preached, people with no explicit faith were still moved by the vision painted by the poetry of his words.

For public policy makers who are or who have been part of a faith community, religious leaders and texts often have moral authority. This provides an organic opening to the raising of moral questions and to attention to the ethical aspects of a problem—particularly when the leader in question is known to be an active participant in their faith. Dr. Salvatierra gives examples of the power of faith to shape legislation in the firsthand accounts described in the following paragraphs.

In 2012 in Kentucky, leaders of evangelical congregations from primarily white, African American, and Latina/o congregations met with Senator Rand Paul, a conversative Christian legislator who had been strongly opposed to immigration reform and in support of more restrictive immigration policy. They gave him the EIT bookmark with forty scriptures that provide insight into immigration and asked him to read one per day and pray about his stance. When they returned at the end of forty days, he shared that he had been affected by the readings and his position had softened.

In central Washington, a series of faith-based experiences led to a major shift in the position of a conservative legislator. I was asked to give an opening biblical reflection at an EIT-sponsored gathering of pastors and legislative leaders for prayer and dialogue. At the beginning of the meeting, there were two participants whose body language showed that they were not fully present—arms folded, looking away. One was the chief of staff of Congressman Dave Reichert, who had been publicly opposed to immigration reform. The other was a representative of the local farmworkers' association, there to recruit clergy for a protest. In my reflection, I spoke about Jesus's call to be as wise as serpents and innocent as doves, saying that dovelike innocence meant keeping an open heart to the movement of the Spirit in people who from a hardheaded perspective are your opponents. Near the end of the gathering, the farmworker representative stood to make her announcement and then suddenly stopped. Addressing the chief of staff by name, she said that she knew that they did not really know one another but that they had certainly seen each other multiple times as the farmworkers protested outside their office. She added that she realized through my reflection that they were both Christians and she had never really thought of anyone in that office as a brother or sister in Christ, that she had a bad heart toward them. With tears in her eyes, and addressing him as a brother, she said that she had decided to trust him as a brother and asked him if she could tell him about the suffering of the members of her church. Shocked, he unfolded his arms, addressed her as a sister, and agreed to listen. Weeping, she went on to tell stories about separated families and destroyed dreams. Afterward, she asked if he would help. He confessed that he did not know very much about the issue but promised to study it and do what he could. A few weeks later, the congressman was at a dinner and seated next to the Evangelical Covenant Church leader for the area in charge of peace and justice ministries. The congressman, also a Christian, shared the story of the change in his chief of staff and asked her to tell him more about the issue. He ended up as one of the strongest Republican voices in Washington supporting immigration reform.

Faith as a Bridge

These stories recounted by Dr. Salvatierra are just a few of the many examples of the particular gifts of faith communities for changing hearts and minds by meeting on common sacred ground. Faith communities are places where people can come together across societal differences through their shared beliefs. Immigrants and nonimmigrants can meet as brothers and sisters in a common faith family. Through faith communities, justice movements have access to people whom they would normally never meet. This capacity for bridge building in and through faith communities is enhanced by traditions of reconciliation that offer strategies and skills for conflict resolution and peacemaking. Working together in joint mission can create life-changing encounters that often result in people engaging in the struggle for justice who otherwise would not be engaged.

Spiritual Sustenance, Healing, and Power

Working for justice is hard, particularly in a struggle that has experienced so little success in the past forty years. Faith communities specialize in spiritual sustenance, creating opportunities for the expression of lament while connecting the weary with hope and support, building resilience in the process. Spiritual perspectives give participants in justice work the long view that makes short-term defeats and losses more bearable. Prayer, at a minimum, changes the person or group that is praying, providing hope and connection to a force larger than themselves in the face of the obstacles that frustrate them. At best, it is a source of additional and real power to impact the situation. Since 2012, the EIT has been leading regular prayer meetings for the pastoral leaders and congregation members in its network. Pastoral leaders are also often invited by immigrant-led organizations to lead prayer before and during actions. Participants in these experiences of fervent prayer testify to the power of the support and emotional healing that they provide in the face of discouragement.

The Unique Gifts of Sanctuary Strategies

The Sanctuary Movement specializes in a unique combination of these characteristics. The ancient Greek saying "those whom the gods would destroy, they first make mad" has particular poignancy at this historical time when a sort of madness has afflicted our body politic. In an episode of mental illness, the sufferer often forgets who they are and whom they belong to. In the same way, many of us have forgotten our common humanity, seeing one another as demons instead of members of the same human family. Pope Francis calls for a "culture of encounter" as the remedy for this ailment, in which we meet God in the other—including those whom we are most likely to see as a threat by virtue of their difference. He identifies migrants as people whom we are most likely to see in distorted ways and with whom a spiritual encounter is most essential.[2] One of the most powerful barriers to the achievement of a more humane, logical, just, and effective immigration system is the visceral response to immigrants, particularly those from the Global South and East, as dangerous others rather than potential sources of contribution and blessing.

The core activity of sanctuary is an encounter in which the immigrant and the native step across the boundary to stand and suffer together. It is a public willingness to enter into risk for the sake of the other, demonstrating their value. Citizens encountering the Sanctuary Movement can no longer say "this is not my problem" because people just like them are seeing that it is our common problem—so much so that they are willing to place their lives on the line. Immigrants encountering the Sanctuary Movement can no longer say, "I have no role in creating change in my new country" because other immigrants are stepping up and risking their personal safety for the possibility of a broader social transformation. At their best, sanctuary strategies that create human connections between immigrants and native-born allies shift the public debate. When Cardinal Roger Mahony preached his Ash Wednesday sermon in 2006, calling for every Catholic to take the risk of potentially violating the law in order to live the gospel in ministering with migrants, he effectively changed the terms of debate.

The act of solidarity at the heart of the Sanctuary Movement also has another powerful dimension. We come to love those whom we invest in sacrificially. Military veterans often talk about the depth and power of the emotional bonds forged between comrades on the battlefield. In sharing the experience of sanctuary, congregations become personally invested in an issue that is often an afterthought in the halls of power. Nonimmigrants become passionate enough to continue advocating even in the face of multiple defeats, and immigrants are strengthened in their conviction that they can achieve their common goals. The opportunity for physical acts of care that congregations provide sets the stage for these relationships and their impact to build over time. Sanctuary at its best provides a core team of passionately committed people who can bring the gifts and contributions of faith to the broader movement for the long haul.

The "air war" power of the moral voice and the "ground war" power of intimate solidarity are combined in the act of sanctuary in ways that fuel and nurture broader activism and help move the dial on pro-immigrant policy.

The Obstacles

The faith community has potential to become a bridge across the contentious divides between moderate and progressive groups within the immigrant rights movement. The historic tools for peacemaking and reconciliation embedded in religious teachings and practices should be useful. However, that has often not occurred. Instead, many leaders, often white leaders, who are engaged in the Sanctuary Movement typically echo the rhetoric and language of the most progressive wings of the movement, sometimes alienating moderate immigrant religious communities. Although the early Sanctuary Movement was ultimately supported by most mainline denominations and many Roman Catholic institutions, in more recent times moderate faith communities have moved away from the word "sanctuary" because of its progressive political and theological associations. At the same time, the more progressive wings of the secular movement are suspicious of the historic domination of primarily white churches and leaders in contexts where these churches and leaders are the ones providing sanctuary resources for vulnerable immigrant families—an automatic power imbalance. The role of immigrant leadership and Central American movement leadership in the earlier Sanctuary Movement was often informal or hidden, partially as a deliberate strategy and partially because the society as a whole did not have the current level of consciousness about power sharing and centering marginalized communities. The New Sanctuary Movement has sought to actively correct this imbalance through structures that give voice and power to sanctuary recipients. However, the theological and political positions and language of many sanctuary leaders are suspect to many of the immigrant-led churches whose participation could enable more effective and organic power sharing. Examples of effective resolution of both these problems can be found in pockets, but the overall challenge remains.

Another challenge for the Sanctuary Movement is the cultural desensitization that has occurred in the age of the internet. When the first sanctuary representatives went to trial in 1985, the images in the press were shocking and powerful to church leaders around the country. In cyberspace, the constant flood of potentially emotive images has reduced their power. Andy Warhol famously said that "in the future, everyone will be world famous for 15 minutes."[3] How can the message of sanctuary have its traditional impact in this modern world of information overload? The grassroots impact of sanctuary also requires a level of personal commitment that the acceleration and disconnected nature of modern life impedes. The activities of sanctuary cannot be carried out online and are time-consuming. Local immigrant rights coalitions still call upon faith-based organizations for needed support, but the unique power of sanctuary is not as evident as it once was.

Religion and Attitudes toward Immigrants and Immigration Reform

As mentioned above, an obstacle to passing comprehensive immigration reform is negative opinions in the U.S. population about immigrants that can be easily stoked by politicians for self-serving reasons. In 1965, the Gallup Organization began asking Americans, "In your view, should immigration be kept at its present level, increased, or decreased." In every year that this question has been asked, the majority of the U.S. population has said that they prefer decreased levels, and in only one year—2010—has the percentage stating they would prefer an increase reached 20 percent (Melkonian-Hoover and Kellstedt 2019). Thus, despite being a "nation of immigrants," most of the U.S. public has consistently opposed increased immigration. In the last thirty years, anti-immigrant sentiment peaked in the early 1990s, then again in the early 2000s following the September 11 attacks, but responses have not changed significantly over the last twenty-five years (Melkonian-Hoover and Kellstedt 2019).

Despite these durable anti-immigrant sentiments, however, surveys from the past ten years consistently show that a majority of U.S. residents, including a majority of believers from all religious groups, support the basic tenets of comprehensive immigration reform. For example, a majority of U.S. residents think that undocumented immigrants should have a path to citizenship and that "dreamers" should be given legal residency (Melkonian-Hoover and Kellstedt 2019). This seems contradictory—that most Americans do not want more immigration, but most also support laws making it possible for undocumented people to become legal residents. Indeed, the general negative attitudes toward immigration in the population make it difficult to pass comprehensive immigration reform, even if a majority of Americans are in favor of specific policies that allow for a path to citizenship, because the fears and anti-immigrant sentiments of the many can be easily stoked by opponents of immigration reform for political gain, as was illustrated during the Trump presidency.

A significant obstacle for *faith-based* mobilizing for immigration reform is that affiliation with Christian congregations, at least for white Christians, has been consistently shown to have a significant negative effect on attitudes toward immigrants and immigration reform. In a comprehensive analysis of national survey data from social scientific sources spanning twenty-five years, Melkonian-Hoover and Kellstedt (2019) found that throughout the past quarter of a century, white evangelical Protestants have been the religious group in the United States most opposed to immigration reform, view the effects of immigration most negatively, and favor the most restrictive immigration policies.[4] For example, white evangelicals are consistently the group most likely to believe that immigrants take jobs from American citizens, increase crime rates, and are a burden to our country and that undocumented immigrants should be deported. White mainline Protestants and white Catholics, however, are not far behind and do not differ significantly from white evangelical Protestants on most of these measures. Emerson and Bracey (2024) found that white practicing Christians in America (defined as people who identify as white, say they are Christians, say their faith is very important to them, and attend church once a month or more), regardless of denominational affiliation, are significantly more likely than the overall U.S. population to state that "immigrants coming into the United States are taking too many jobs from U.S. citizens" and significantly less likely than the overall U.S. population to say that "we should have laws in the US to protect immigrants from being treated unjustly."

When comparing racial/religious groups in their attitudes toward immigration, Melkonian-Hoover and Kellstedt (2019) found that within every racial/ethnic group, being self-identified as a Christian, especially being self-identified as evangelical, leads to more negative views toward immigrants compared to those with no religious affiliation or those identifying as Muslim, Jewish, or Buddhist. They found that white evangelicals hold the most negative views of immigrants and favor the most restrictive policies. Latino and Asian evangelicals are much more likely to have positive views of immigrants than their white evangelical counterparts but are less favorable toward immigrants and immigration reform compared to other religious groups (such as Jews, Buddhists, and Muslims) within their respective racial/ethnic groups. Interestingly, across all racial/ethnic groups agnostics and atheists are the religious group most positive toward immigrants and the most favorable toward more generous immigration policies. Jews and Muslims, however, were close behind agnostics and atheists in having the most positive views toward immigrants and immigration reform (Melkonian-Hoover and Kellstedt 2019).

All of this suggests the following: practicing white Christians, especially white evangelicals, are the group least likely to support immigrants and policies favorable toward them. This is despite the fact that religious teachings in all Christian traditions are overwhelmingly in favor of welcoming and protecting foreigners. These facts illustrate the challenge of centering immigration protection and advocacy work within religious organizations, particularly Christian organizations, in the United States.

However, Melkonian-Hoover and Kellstedt (2019) also found that clergy are on average more favorable toward immigrants and immigration reform than their congregation members. In addition, lay members, regardless of denomination, who reported that their clergy spoke about immigration from the pulpit, and especially when churches have programs aimed at helping immigrants, are more likely to have positive views of immigrants and immigration reform compared to those whose clergy never have spoken about immigration. They also found, however, that the great majority of all clergy in all Christian denominations, across all racial/ethnic groups, do not ever speak of immigration from the pulpit. As we will see, the fear of raising conflict within the congregation keeps many clergy from speaking out about this contentious issue.

It is not clear, then, why Christians of all races/ethnicities in the United States tend to be more negative toward immigrants and immigration reform than religiously nonaffiliated people, Jews, Buddhists, and Muslims when most Christian clergy never speak publicly about immigration in their congregations. This would require an entire book-length research project to unpack. These findings do clearly show, however, that Christian clergy who are willing to take the risk to speak out about immigration justice in their congregations, and to start programs within their churches to provide aid or advocacy for immigrants, can have a tremendous influence in reversing the negative views of their members. Christian clergy are therefore uniquely situated to convince the most anti-immigrant residents in the United States to change their views. U.S. religion is thus simultaneously an obstacle to and a potential catalyst for the movement to advocate for immigrants and immigration reform.

Conclusion

Sanctuary movements and broader faith-based immigrant justice initiatives have historically played a powerful role in public policy change, rooted in shifts in public debate and opinion as well as changes in the perspectives of members of local congregations and faith leaders. Sanctuary's impact has been an important component in the overall role of faith leaders, communities, and institutions in the context of the broad movement for immigrant justice. This impact has resulted from its dramatic demonstration of risky, intimate solidarity across the line between immigrant and citizen. Sanctuary has embodied an inspiring moral message with emotional and spiritual power that has influenced believers and those with a resonant ethical framework. The movement, however, is encountering significant challenges in the current political climate that will require fundamental changes to meet.

Faith-based organizations play a significant and unique role in the larger immigrant rights movement by offering certain resources that secular organizations generally do not provide. First of all, they contribute inspiring moral language of a higher law of love that motivates both activists and policy makers of faith toward more moral, compassionate, and just treatment of immigrants. Second, they provide hope and sustenance to keep people working toward this goal amid frustrations and in the absence of progress. Third, they have the capacity to be bridging institutions, connecting immigrants with nonimmigrants and laypeople with activists and decisionmakers by virtue of their common faith. Secular activists realize these unique capacities and are for the most part happy to work with faith-based organizations to do the types of work that they are less equipped to do.

Despite these unique gifts and contributions, faith-based organizations also bring their own constraints to the work of organizing for immigrant rights. Cultural and theological differences often make it difficult to unify members of different religious traditions and racial/ ethnic groups. In fact, cultural differences are often framed in religious and theological terms, making compromise more difficult. In addition, the anti-immigrant sentiments of a large percentage of lay members of congregations that faith-based organizers are trying to mobilize make it difficult for pastors and priests to engage in supporting any movements for immigrant rights for fear of alienating large parts of their constituencies.

One explanation for the anti-immigrant sentiments, particularly among white U.S. Christians, is the legacy of the dominance of European American Christian institutions in the United States and their influence on the perspectives of their members, regardless of racial and ethnic background. For most of U.S. history, the most dominant European American religious institutions have theologically legitimated white supremacist doctrines such as the doctrine of discovery, manifest destiny, race-based slavery, and racial segregation.

Thus, these institutions for much of their history have taken for granted the idea that white European American rule over the continent and its borders is not only legitimate but God's will because of the superiority of Christianity and European culture. These ideas then lead to the sentiment that immigrants of color are somehow an inferior population and that for immigration to be legitimate it must benefit the white majority. As we will see, the legacy and influence of European American–dominated Christianity is often an obstacle to advocating for and protecting immigrants. This highlights the importance of having immigrant faith leaders at the center of the movement.

Despite this legacy, however, clergy of all racial/ethnic groups who are willing to take seriously the strong official teachings of the Christian religion to welcome, support, and advocate for immigrants appear to have tremendous potential to change the views of their members. In addition, as history reveals, the ability of religious institutions to mobilize people has proven to be a powerful resource for social change. Thus, religion in the United States serves simultaneously as a powerful resource and an obstacle for movements advocating for more welcoming and humane policies for immigrants.

3

Accompaniment

Sergio Flores, an asylum seeker currently living in suburban Los Angeles, is a father of three and comes from a small village in Honduras.[1] This village, like many in Honduras, has a prominent presence of organized crime. *Las maras* (gangs) control the village and require extortion "tax" payments for the "protection" of family members. Because of Sergio's intermittent and unstable employment as a farmhand, his ability to pay the extortion was inconsistent, often resulting in threats of violence to his family. During one such period in 2014, his wife took his newborn daughter and fled to the United States for safety, leaving Sergio to care for his older daughter and son. His wife crossed the border without authorization and found work near her brother in a small town in the southeastern United States. In 2018, four years after his wife and newborn daughter fled, Sergio was beaten severely by members of *la mara* for failure to pay his extortion tax:

> I was behind in my payments; I couldn't pay them and they found me at the soccer field and we started arguing and I told them that I couldn't keep paying because I didn't have a job. They attacked me there with stones and hurt me badly and I had to be taken to the hospital. As soon as I was transferred from the hospital, I didn't go back to the village. They threatened my son too. They wanted him to distribute drugs. There was another person who said horrible things to my [then twelve-year-old] daughter. She almost didn't tell me because they said "if you tell him we'll kill him by skinning him." But in the end, she told me. After that I told her that I'd get her out of there and take her away.

After these incidents in 2018, Sergio left for the U.S. border with his two children (ages twelve and seventeen) to try to reunite with his wife and youngest daughter. He presented himself on the U.S. side of a border crossing in the Southwest with his children to seek asylum. He was immediately separated from his children. Both Sergio and his children were placed in detention centers, and soon after Sergio was deported back to Honduras without his children.

This was during the Trump administration's "zero-tolerance" policy in 2018. More than 2,700 children were separated from their asylum-seeking parents along the border in 2018 according to the Department of Health and Human Services. Hundreds of parents, including Sergio, were deported without their children. The U.S. government in many cases lost track of which child belonged to which parent and, like happened to Sergio, sent parents back to Central America without telling them where their children were (Sieff and Kinosian 2019).

Sergio describes the experience:

It was terrible when they took away my kids. Because that was a moment, I didn't know what to do, because they treated me poorly at that moment when they took away my kids, they began to tell me, "look, we are going to charge you and you are going back to Honduras, you will never see your children again." There were many terrible things there, and they did not care. They would see a mother throwing herself on the floor when they took her son away—I still see that as if I were looking at you—the mother was begging them not to take the child away from her. The immigration officer was holding the hand of the child and they did not care to see the pain of the mother. Then at that terrible moment in the separation, you were treated like an animal, they said terrible things to you.

Sergio describes his life back in Honduras without his children:

When I arrived back at the house in Honduras, I arrived at the house and I hadn't talked to my children, and they're not with me. They're not with you, and you think, where are they? That moment was the most terrible. Even more so when you're coming home every day, you know that your children are not there. My mind works every day, minute by second, where are they? You want to know about them. Yes, it affects you psychologically, the thing that affects you most is the separation.

I was shocked, I did not remember things sometimes because I was traumatized. I could hear the screams of children at night, which was terrible. A young man who was in the same detention center, where I was, hung himself in the icebox [main area of detention center kept at fifty-five degrees]. When they separated him [from his son], he knew he definitely wasn't going to see his son so he killed himself.

After returning to Honduras, Sergio had to move from village to village, staying with friends and family to avoid *la mara*. His children were housed in a detention center for children in the United States during this time. After a few months, he was contacted over the phone by Al Otro Lado, a Tijuana-based nonprofit legal service organization advocating for immigrants. Al Otro Lado worked with the ACLU to identify parents in Central America who had been deported without their children. Through funding raised by many immigrant rights organizations, such as Families Belong Together and Together Rising, Al Otro Lado set out to find as many of these parents as they could. They identified twenty-nine parents in Honduras, Guatemala, and El Salvador who, like Sergio, had presented themselves near the border to apply for asylum or were apprehended while crossing the border and then were deported without their children. Al Otro Lado paid for their travel expenses to a hotel in Tijuana to work on their legal cases to be reunified with their children and apply for asylum. Al Otro Lado contacted faith leaders and organizations in the United States, including Matthew 25 / Mateo 25, We Care, and CLUE, to help accompany the families and to find host homes and sponsors willing to be financially responsible for the parents for six months while in the United States during the reunification process. The network of faith-based organizations and leaders was able to secure offers for over fifty sponsors and hosts all over the nation in less than forty-eight hours.

On Saturday, March 2, 2019, these twenty-nine families, including parents and children, converged on the small border town of Mexicali along with dozens of advocates—including their Al Otro Lado lawyers and faith leaders from numerous organizations to accompany them—to attempt to cross the border to be reunified with their children. They chose the Mexicali border crossing because it has less traffic and they reasoned that they would have a better chance of being processed there. They gathered at a hotel lobby near the border with all of their luggage. Faith leaders led the families in prayer for safety and reunification and led them in spiritual hymns as they prepared to attempt to cross the border. Hope, angst, and joy filled the air.

On the U.S. side of the border in Calexico, a group of fifteen or so Southern California–based faith leaders gathered to pray in front of the border crossing processing building, asking God for his justice to be done and to "free the captives" on the other side of the building. Faith leaders were invited by Al Otro Lado as an advocacy strategy. It was believed that clergy represented a nonviolent, moral presence that could uniquely persuade those in authority. As the twenty-nine families presented themselves at the border with all of their documentation and paperwork meticulously prepared in organized packets by Al Otro Lado lawyers, the Customs and Border Protection (CBP) officials denied entry to the twenty-nine families, saying that there was no capacity to house them in a nearby detention center. The lawyers made their case that refusing to allow them to enter would violate a recent federal court ruling, which mandated that the families separated at the border under the zero-tolerance policy be reunified. The CBP was unmoved, stating that they needed to wait on the Mexican side of the border until capacity at detention centers opened up. Several faith leaders on the U.S. side asked to see the director of the border processing facility. The director was willing to take a phone call from LA Episcopal bishop John Taylor and Jack Miranda, an evangelical pastor and activist from Los Angeles County. They urged the director to do what was right and just in God's eyes, allowing the families to be reunited. The national press had a large presence at the border crossing as well, as they were notified by the leaders organizing the crossing. By midmorning stories of the attempted crossing had been posted on the front page of the *NBC News* and *Washington Post* websites, adding to the pressure of the moment.

By early evening the CBP finally relented and began processing the families five at a time, allowing them to cross the border. Most were sent to detention centers in other cities. Sergio was one of those sent to a detention center for two months while his case was being processed. During this time, he learned that his children were released from their detention center and reunited with their mother in the Southeast. After two months in detention, Sergio was released and was assigned to immigration court in California. He lived with a host family associated with Matthew 25 / Mateo 25 in the Los Angeles area while his asylum case was in process. When we last spoke to him, he remained separated from his children because he needed to be near his immigration court in California so that he could appear at a moment's notice for hearings and check-ins with ICE and had no money to travel because he was not authorized to work. He spoke with his children regularly on WhatsApp but missed them greatly. He was working toward trying to visit them for Christmas.

Sergio's story highlights the trauma resulting from the Trump administration's zero-tolerance policy, and the network of organizations mobilizing to address the detentions and family separations carried out by the U.S. government. Legal aid organizations, like the ACLU and Al Otro Lado, worked in concert with faith-based organizations, like Matthew 25 / Mateo 25, CLUE, and We Care, to coordinate both legal assistance and accompaniment. This chapter highlights the work of faith-based organizations to accompany immigrants in detention, in the face of deportation, and as they worked to reunify their families and gain legal residency during the Trump administration's immigration crackdown.

Defining Accompaniment

Different organizations have different definitions of immigration accompaniment. For some, it means primarily accompanying immigrants to court hearings, border crossings, and ICE check-ins. Having a person, particularly an English-speaking member of the dominant culture, can make a significant difference in the treatment that immigrants receive by ICE, CBP, and immigration judges. The story recounted of the border crossing in Mexicali/Calexico illustrates this type of accompaniment. It is unlikely that CBP would have begun processing the cases of the twenty-nine families without community members accompanying them and pressuring CBP to allow them to cross. A broader definition of accompaniment includes helping immigrants access basic needs like housing, child care, medical care, food, and nonlegal logistical support as well as giving spiritual and emotional support to those walking the long, difficult journey of the legal processes involved in seeking asylum and/or legal residency. We use this broader definition of accompaniment in our analysis because most of the faith leaders and organizations we studied are involved in much more than ICE check-ins, court hearings, and border accompaniment.

Three Models of Accompaniment

In our analysis of our in-depth interviews of faith-based organizations doing immigration accompaniment, we found three broad and somewhat overlapping models of accompaniment, all of which have challenges and advantages. We have labeled the three models (1) *flexible networks*, (2) *support circles*, and (3) *place-based* accompaniment models. We highlight an example of one organization effectively utilizing each model.

Flexible Networks: We Care

The flexible network model refers to the accompaniment of vulnerable immigrants through broad informal networks of individuals and organizations that combine and recombine for short-term, often onetime tasks. In the early days of the Trump administration's rapidly changing policy, most faith-based organizations utilized this model of accompaniment. Policies were changing so rapidly that prompt response networks of anyone willing to help provide housing, watch children, or accompany people to court or ICE check-ins were mobilized through a network of volunteers through social media and email. As mistakes were made and challenges better understood, some organizations altered this strategy to become more structured and organized.

We Care is an example of an organization that continues to use the flexible network model effectively. We Care has become one of the most effective faith-based organizations in the nation accompanying asylum seekers. During the years 2018 to 2020, it secured the release of more than a hundred asylum seekers from detention, found sponsors and housing, and provided food, transportation, and legal assistance to all of them. This is quite surprising because We Care is largely the work of just one husband-and-wife team, Ada and Melvin Valiente, who are also copastors of First Baptist Church of Maywood in the Los Angeles area. Ada also works full-time as a social worker. We Care is officially incorporated as a 501(c)(3) nonprofit organization but operates primarily as the catalyst to mobilize a national network of (mostly) immigrant congregations, individuals, legal aid organizations, and other faith-based nonprofit organizations to accompany asylum seekers. We Care has no regular source of revenue but is able to raise funds quickly through its national network. We Care also has no staff—the pastors simply mobilize their network for the completion of specific tasks. Its strength lies in the breadth of the networks of these two pastors, who are well known in both U.S. Latina/o and Central American church circles.

We Care was founded when the Valientes were contacted and asked to help a woman asylum seeker who had fled Nicaragua because her son was killed by the government for participating in a peaceful protest. Her life was in danger, and she presented herself at the border to ask for asylum but was sent to a detention center in the United States. Because of their connection to churches in Nicaragua (Ada is Nicaraguan), the Valientes were contacted and were able to get the woman released from detention while she worked on her asylum case. This case was broadcast throughout Central America by CNN en Español and Telemundo. As a result of this publicity, the Valientes became known throughout Central America. When migrants who have heard about the Valientes come to the border seeking asylum, they often contact the pastors through their website or Facebook page asking for help. Typically, the pastors will respond within a few days and have a phone conversation. If the case will plausibly result in a successful asylum claim, they will activate their national network to try to (1) get legal assistance, (2) raise money for bond out of detention, (3) find a sponsor to be financially responsible for the asylum seeker, (4) find a family to host the person while their asylum case is being heard, and (5) help the person find financial resources for living expenses, rides to court, and eventually jobs to help support themselves while their case is being heard.

The pastors are highly networked with other organizations, including legal aid and immigrant rights associations, universities, and other churches and faith-based groups. When they agree to take on a case, they immediately send out a message in a chat on the social media app Signal and typically a lawyer will respond and be willing to take the case either pro bono or at a reduced cost. They then send out requests over Signal, social media, and their personal email network for donations to cover legal expenses and to find a legal sponsor. If the person is eligible for bond during the time their case is being heard, they send out another request to cover the cost. Once the person is set to be released, they send out a request for someone to host the person for six months in their home, along with financial assistance for travel and getting started in the United States. Typically, the person is placed within a week of being released. During the years 2018 to 2020 We Care facilitated the release of over a hundred asylum seekers, all of whom had a legal sponsor and were hosted by a family and most of whom had legal representation to argue their asylum cases. The strength of this organization is clearly the wide national networks of these two pastors, rather than formal structures or funding. Those hosting the individuals are usually either extended family members of the asylum seeker or individuals from U.S. Latina/o immigrant congregations. The host usually commits to housing the asylum seeker for six months, but it often lasts longer. Typically, the host is part of an immigrant congregation that helps out with supporting the asylum seeker, but there are no formal structures in place to organize support.

Pastor Ada explains the network approach:

> We are on Signal and this is national—you're going to find people from all over the United States, even some in Mexico. And we put our needs there. There are a lot of people on Signal and they only put people [in the Signal chat] that they trust. So, I was invited to be part of that about a year and a half ago because they saw me put in a lot of requests so they connected with me. And they said, pastor Ada, you know we want you to be part of our group.
>
> We have a team that does document translation for the asylum seekers. Everything needs to be translated. One of them is based in Houston, the other one is based in Miami. So, we send them all the documentation. These are professionals specialized just in translation. They donate their time and they do all the translations. We have two people. I never met them personally but we do it all through WhatsApp and Zoom. But these are Nicaraguan volunteers—they know the situation in Nicaragua so we utilize them because they know the political issues. So, they text us, pastor can I help with this? Can we network with you? Sure. So, that's how the resources come. You know, somebody can get the airline tickets, somebody's going to go pick them up or somebody can help you pay the bond.

According to the leaders of We Care, they have nearly a 100 percent success rate in getting asylum seekers out of detention. One of the asylum seekers whom We Care served was amazed at the resources that they were able to assemble on his behalf through this informal network:

> The first step we took was that they got me a lawyer then they got me a sponsor because I came with nothing. She said, "Do not worry, we have a good team, we will help you." And they got me the sponsor and then when they set my bail at five thousand dollars, I was like what do I do? In Nicaragua it is not easy to get five thousand. And thank God with the pastor she had RAICES (Texas-based legal aid nonprofit) pay the bail. They also provided me with their home. I came to live with them—I don't pay rent. They gave me their home, food, everything I might need. And now we are working in the legal process. I have received support to work legally, to walk in health, where I am living, food, and clothes. I also have support in my Christian path, how to be a better Christian.

The Christian support of prayer and emotional care was central to the accompaniment of many of the immigrants we interviewed, most of whom have a strong personal faith commitment.

Typically, We Care handles the cases of around twenty asylum seekers at a time. Part of the reason for their high success rate is that they take on only cases that appear to have legitimate asylum claims. According to Pastor Melvin, "Usually, we take the cases that are applying for asylum. If somebody is here because they just want to find a job or they don't have a good source of income in their countries and they apply for asylum, we are honest with them and we tell them 'no that doesn't qualify.' But those who qualify for asylum, usually we are able to get 100 percent out." These leaders claim that if an asylum claim is legitimate and they are able to secure legal assistance, almost all are released from detention while their cases are processed. The problem for most asylum seekers who are not released is the lack of legal representation and a sponsor and host while their cases are being processed.

The leaders of We Care also claim that the fact that they are Baptist pastors helps them gain trust with ICE officials, especially those in the Bible Belt.

So especially in Texas—which you would think would be the toughest—the advantage of Texas is that they have a lot of people who are Christians working with ICE. So, when we call them and they know that we're pastors, immediately, they show respect and they listen to us and they work with us. So probably that's one of the reasons why we are successful. So being pastors, having good communication skills and knowing, knowing how to work the system, that's what helps.

The pastors emphasized that they try to build relationships with the ICE officials, speak respectfully to them, and convey that their faith has led them to help people with their asylum cases.

Another possible reason for the high success rate is that most (around 70 percent) of the cases taken by We Care are asylum seekers from Nicaragua who are fleeing for political reasons. Since the U.S. government has a hostile relationship with the Nicaraguan government, ICE has been more amenable to hearing their asylum claims. However, 30 percent of We Care's cases are from El Salvador and Honduras, where asylum seekers are fleeing gang violence rather than political persecution. We Care claims to have secured release from detention nearly all of those cases as well. Melvin Valiente explains,

> So, in Honduras, usually we take the cases of people who will be killed by gang members if they return and they already have been threatened that they're going to be killed. So, in those cases we help them. For example, two daughters of pastors were living in El Salvador and gang members threatened to kill them because they didn't want to go out with them. And she had written notices that she was going to be killed and she came asking for asylum. So, we were able to get the two of them out. And also, another person was a lawyer working for one of the government offices and she said she was working on one of the gang cases and they wanted to kill her. And so, she had to flee the country and we were able to get her out of detention.

Often it takes more than a year to process the cases, and the immigration courts at the time were moving very slowly because of the backlog caused by the COVID-19 pandemic. Some will likely take multiple years to resolve. Central to the success of getting asylum seekers out of detention has been the ability of We Care to secure legal assistance through their continually expanding informal networks of pro bono and low-bono lawyers all over the country. One particularly fruitful connection is a partnership with the law school at the University of Oklahoma. Pastor Ada explains,

> When we had the first case in Oklahoma, I didn't have money. So, I started calling Catholic Charities and different places and in one of those calls somebody said "call the University of Oklahoma. They have a group there who does work with immigration." So, I call this person, and she was very nice and she said, "Oh yeah, pastor, anything you need, we can help you. Yeah. We have people who are graduating every year from the immigration law school and one of the requirements is that they do some practice." And so, she gave me her number and everything and she said, "Anytime you need something, call me." And I'm really here to help. So, she is one of our contacts now. And so, in terms of how many people help those who we constantly call, it's probably about forty lawyers nationally.

In addition to securing legal assistance, We Care advises and educates some asylum seekers before they present themselves at the border. According to Pastor Melvin,

> What we learned in those cases is how important consistency is in the way they present their cases. So, whatever they said first they need to keep the same story because they interview them three times. So, if those three stories are different, then that makes the path harder. So, what we're learning is that these judges are fair. But they don't like anybody to lie to them. They're nice but they don't take lies. So, we train people to never lie and to have consistency in their stories and not to give a lot of dates because they might get confused and contradict themselves.

Advice like this is a central part of the accompaniment that We Care provides. In some cases, in which they can't find a pro bono attorney for them, the pastors walk the asylum seeker through their legal paperwork themselves.

We Care also helps asylum seekers secure housing, food, sponsors, and employment for those released from detention while they are waiting for their asylum cases. Since their work began in 2018, the Valientes have had asylum seekers living in their own home and have worked to find housing for all of the others they were able to get released from detention, which is the most difficult task. Asylum seekers often need housing for more than a year while they wait for their cases to be resolved. In most of those cases they have no money to pay rent because they are not allowed to work legally. The pastors who lead We Care have a family-first approach to securing housing.

> How do we find homes for them? First of all, when they come to us, we ask if they have a place to stay, they say, "No, we don't have anybody to stay with." At first, they don't want to bother their family. So now by experience, we know that. So, we tried to push it a little bit harder and they will find somebody who is a relative. We say, "Maybe you have a friend, maybe you have a relative here, and give me a phone number of somebody in Nicaragua or Honduras that we can call to talk to." So, we try to connect with their families and most of them say, "Oh, I have a cousin there, or I have an uncle there." So, we start calling them first and we say, "We don't even know him and we're trying to help him. And he's your nephew. So, if he's your nephew, your sister's son, I think you should help us because we don't even know who he is. You're helping him. You're doing it. You are closer. You should probably do it." If they have to say no, that's fine. But we're willing to put it this way. But we are able to find people who are able to host them if they really don't have anybody. We post it on social media and we find people usually. They say we are willing to help have them for six months. So, we call them and we say, we have a home for six months.

This family-based approach seems to be the most effective and has led to approximately half of the asylum seekers they have aided finding housing through extended family. However, they have been able to find hosts for over fifty people with nonrelatives as well. These homes are typically found through posting the need on Signal or through emails to their networks of volunteers, most of whom are in U.S. Latina/o congregations.

We Care activates a network of organizations for simpler needs, like food and money for plane tickets, clothes, and transportation to and from airports.

The American Baptist Churches denomination—they help us buy plane tickets and they help us with transportation. They say, anytime you need somebody to go take them to the airport, call and we'll send somebody. We network sometimes with LA Voice and CLUE. They sometimes provide money for legal assistance or plane tickets. And then our church, sometimes we need a home for a week or two weeks and, and I would announce that at church and we usually find one or two homes. So, what made us successful besides the help of God, which is the most important, is the ability to network with organizations.

While the flexible network model is effective for We Care, its success may be difficult to replicate for a number of reasons. We Care's pastors are unique in their wide national network of relationships with other U.S. Latina/o and Central American pastors. They are also unique in that one of the pastors, Ada, is also a social worker and therefore has wide networks among nonprofits, service providers, and government agencies. She also understands the legal processes surrounding immigration. Another reason for their success in getting asylum seekers released is their screening process—they take only cases that have a high likelihood of success, and many of the cases are referred to them by their church networks in Nicaragua. This allows them to screen out cases that are not likely to succeed. Last, a majority of the asylum seekers they have accompanied are from Nicaragua and are fleeing political persecution; their asylum cases are looked upon more favorably because of the poor relationship between the Nicaraguan and U.S. governments. Despite these unique factors, it is remarkable that two full-time pastors of a medium-sized church, one of whom has another full-time job as a social worker, could over the course of two years successfully assist in the release of over a hundred asylum seekers from detention and secure sponsors, host homes, and legal representation just through mobilizing their informal networks of pastors, laypeople, nonprofit organizations, and attorneys.

The advantage of using this network-based model is its flexibility and quick response, particularly in an unstable, quickly changing policy environment. Resources and people can be mobilized quickly at virtually any location in the country through digital media for a wide range of short-term tasks, from picking up an asylum seeker at the airport to finding a host family and filing legal documents.

While We Care leverages this model masterfully, this model also has downsides, particularly in the area of hosting asylum seekers in homes. Not all hastily arranged home stays have gone well for other organizations that have used this model. We Care's screening process helps them place asylum seekers who are likely to succeed in the environments in which they are placed, so they have had relatively successful hosting situations. Also, asylum seekers placed with family members are more likely to have a successful transition while being hosted. However, other organizations we studied using the flexible network model have less of a screening process and have had numerous difficult hosting situations. The following story illustrates how things can go wrong.

Stephanie Mc Reynolds and her husband Mark volunteered to host an asylum seeker at their home in a middle-class suburb of Los Angeles.[2] They are part of a loose network of leaders and organizations finding homes for asylum seekers while they wait for their cases. Stephanie and Mark had hosted short-term asylum seekers waiting to move to their permanent locations and had hosted families for up to three weeks. Stephanie was contacted by a nonprofit organization in this loose network and was told of the situation of Carlos, a man in his forties, and his sixteen-year-old son Daniel who needed a long-term place to stay while his asylum case was being processed. Stephanie and Mark both work full-time and have adult children, so they have several empty rooms in their house that they wanted to use to host asylum seekers. They agreed to host Carlos and Daniel for six months. One evening they got a call that Carlos and Daniel were released from detention in San Diego and were on a train to come to live with them. Stephanie and Mark were able to drop what they were doing at a moment's notice and pick them up at the train station.

Stephanie and Mark do not speak any Spanish, and Carlos and Daniel, from rural Honduras, do not speak any English, and Carlos is not able to read, so communication was difficult. Stephanie was connected to several different faith-based nonprofits protecting immigrants, so she called one of their leaders for help with the hosting process. They provided a Spanish-speaking staff person to help with translation and understanding the specifics and logistics of the upcoming court dates and appointments for Carlos and Daniel. According to Stephanie,

> One of the biggest needs was daytime transportation because we worked. And so, you've got to have doctors' appointments, you've got to get them on MediCal. You've got to take them to these ICE meetings . . . and then getting them work. And that became a real, real problem because with the [Trump] administration they just aren't giving work permits. And so, there were things like that. I would say the frustration was that there just wasn't enough of an infrastructure for support [from the organization]. That we thought we had, so that was really hard.

Carlos then began to slide into depression and began to drink heavily. He has five additional children and a wife who live in Honduras. His plan was to support them and send money home, but he couldn't work because he was not able to get a work permit. Federal law requires that asylum seekers wait 150 days before they can apply for a work permit; in 2020 President Trump increased this period to 365 days. Applications can take months, sometimes over a year to be processed. Stephanie described the situation this way:

> Carlos had five children and a wife still at home in Honduras. So, he wanted to get work and send money home. But he couldn't get work. So, he started drinking and he was not functional. So, he would come home and pass out and throw up. He would come in the middle of dinner and grab pots and pans and Daniel was there, you know, his son. And it was tough. And mainly he just wasn't flourishing. . . . I mean he was just falling into pieces. And then he started stealing alcohol from my son. And then he would apologize . . . but there was no life here.

Carlos's drinking seems to have been a way to deal with isolation and lack of communal support. In addition, class and cultural differences made it difficult for Stephanie and Mark to connect with Carlos.

> One of the things that was obviously true was in Honduras, he was basically an indentured servant. So, he had worked for an American guy I guess that owns a huge ranchero in Honduras, and it appears that Carlos

and his entire family lived on this ranchero working and were kind of indentured servants. And so, what Carlos knew to do, the way I think he had survived his whole life, was to figure out what the boss-man wanted and to please him. And so immediately upon moving in he started referring to Mark and I as his mother and father and my son as his brother and stuff. I think he wanted to serve, he wanted to please Mark. Well, this is the cultural difference. The only thing that would have pleased Mark would have been for this person to be self-initiating and get out there and learn English, and he was just incapable of that. That just wasn't who he was. So, part of what was frustrating for us, and I think was a problem for him, was there wasn't anything in place. So [the nonprofit] had gotten these people here, but they didn't really have any plan for how they were going to make it here.

Eventually, after six difficult months, Stephanie and Mark asked Carlos and Daniel to leave, even though Carlos's case was still pending and a long time from being resolved. This was a difficult decision for Stephanie: "Like I said he was not a well-functioning alcoholic. He knew that basically he was going to need to leave. And he didn't want to and he was crying and saying he was sorry, but I just had to hold him and say you cannot stay; you cannot stay and it killed me."

Stephanie blames two primary reasons for this difficult situation that didn't work out. First of all, the network of leaders, nonprofits, and providers that were arranging accompaniment through flexible networks had no plan to connect Carlos and Daniel to a community where they could thrive. They were isolated in a suburban home in a predominantly white neighborhood with nobody around who spoke Spanish. Second, Carlos was not allowed to work because he had no work permit, and if he did work, he knew it would endanger his asylum case. This isolation and lack of ability to provide for himself and his family led to depression and ultimately abusive drinking. Hastily arranged home stays were common by organizations using flexible network approaches to accompaniment. According to Stephanie,

[This nonprofit] has a reputation for playing fast and loose. I think sometimes there were things that would get communicated to people to hosts like us that either were hopeful inspirational comments or "I will say anything I have to say to make sure we have a home for these people." I know the love and care they had. But I think it was unclear why they didn't have more of a plan or at least some idea of how you were going to help these people actually make it once you got them here. These people were in the system and because they were asylum seekers, if they work without a permit, they jeopardize their case. And so, they were in a catch-22. They have to work, I mean, and Carlos in particular because his family was still there. So, he was getting phone calls all the time from his family about stuff they were going through, right? So, a lot of pressure to work, right? And also, it'd be good for them to work, right? And yet if they do that, then they're jeopardizing their case. So, this was the problem.

These problems of lack of community, lack of ability to work, and cultural divides were common among many organizations finding homes for hosting asylum seekers.

Support Circles: Matthew 25 / Mateo 25

Matthew 25 / Mateo 25 leaders had seen many hosting situations arranged by organizations using flexible networks go bad, including one that resulted in violence against the host. As a result, they set out to create a more intentionally organized system of hosting and accompaniment. Their approach represents our second model of accompaniment.

In response to the need to have a more organized system of hosting and support, Matthew 25 / Mateo 25 developed a system of "support circles," partnerships of multiple congregations, both immigrant and nonimmigrant, who agree to host and accompany an asylum seeker. A leader of Matthew 25 / Mateo 25 explained the need for a more organized system of hosting and accompaniment: "Everybody is getting called and the whole thing is a mess, right? Because [different organizations] are throwing people in homes who have said yes with no support and no rules and no structure and some people are getting burned out and crazy things are happening." In response, Matthew 25 / Mateo 25 organized a number of denominational leaders in Southern California to donate money to hire an intake coordinator and to recruit congregations from their denominations to commit to hosting and accompanying an asylum seeker. This network of congregations and denominations became known as the Ecumenical Coalition for Asylum Seekers (ECAS), a subgroup under the umbrella of Matthew 25 / Mateo 25. Key to the strategy of ECAS support circles is pairing immigrant and nonimmigrant congregations to do the work together, with the immigrant congregation taking the lead and providing a community of support for the asylum seeker. At the core of Matthew 25 / Mateo 25's values is the idea that those most affected by the injustice they are addressing, in this case immigrants, are centered in leadership and organization. A leader of Matthew 25 / Mateo 25 explains it this way:

> ECAS is all about support circles, but it's not done like traditional refugee resettlement. Traditional refugee resettlement is racist. You know, it hinders people, right? So, we do it Mateo 25 style, which means that immigrant and nonimmigrant churches are together in the support circle. And because of that, the whole dynamic shifts. There's a covenant between the guest and the host and there's a covenant between the guest and support circle and the support team does not take responsibility for the guest and the guest does not have to do what the support team wants them to do. So, if the guest doesn't want to learn English, they don't have to learn English. Right? But on the other hand, when the three months are up the three months are up because we're not taking responsibility.

This leader then explained three stages of accompaniment in an ECAS support circle:

> There's an initial stage where we do everything for the person. We're all involved. We do everything for the person, we're their family. . . . Then the second stage is to support the person in finding where they want to live their lives in this new country. So, the immigrant churches and the circle are critically important because they operate like older brothers and sisters. You know, this is how to use public transportation. This is where the stores are, this is how to get a job, my cousin has a job for you, you know, and then stage 3 is that you give back—you're part of the support circle, not as a guest, but as a contributor.

The uniqueness of this Matthew 25 / Mateo 25 support circle model is the intentional pairing of immigrant and nonimmigrant congregations, and the immigrant congregation plays the key role in transitioning the asylum seeker into their new lives. The reason for incorporating non-immigrant congregations in accompaniment is the pursuit of the larger goal of building support for compassionate immigration reform among white Christians, who are a key political obstacle in passing immigration reform. The strategy, therefore, is to "convert" nonimmigrant evangelical Christians toward a passion for immigration reform by connecting them with the real lives of immigrants and immigrant fellow Christian believers.

In Matthew 25 / Mateo 25 support circles, the nonimmigrant congregation may contribute the room to live in and financial resources, but the immigrant congregation provides the community support. In the story of Carlos above, it was the lack of community connection and ability to work that left him isolated and depressed. One asylum seeker hosted by a Matthew 25 / Mateo 25 support circle expressed appreciation for this community support provided by the congregations in their support circle:

> I think that is the best thing they are doing, opening their doors to help the neighbor when you need it most, because the migrant comes empty-handed to this place without knowing a language without knowing people and they, thank God, open the doors helping us to integrate into the society of this country, how everything works. They have taught us to use a subway or how to use the bus, how to use the laundromat. They have taken the support they are giving us very seriously. When my daughter turned fifteen, they even gave her a *quinceañera* party.

The Matthew 25 / Mateo 25 support circle model also includes a peer-based trauma care model. Therapist Michelle Jimenez in collaboration with ECAS coordinator Luis Gonzalez provided both individual one-on-one sessions and weekly group trauma care sessions. In the weekly group sessions, asylum seekers accompanied and supported each other in walking through their trauma and reaching their goals. They also received training in life skills for the United States and leadership development workshops, including workshops from some of the members of the group in areas where they had particular expertise. Jimenez and Gonzalez are immigrants themselves and experienced significant trauma as a part of their personal journeys; this helped support the leadership of the members of the group as they could identify with the caregivers. Jimenez focused on pastoral care and emotional support integrating spiritual and psychological care, but her background in play therapy in Costa Rica helped with the group process. Once a month, all the participants and volunteers went on an outing—a family fun day—which helped the members of the group to see themselves as part of a family rather than seeing themselves only through the lenses of their trauma.

Many migrants experience trauma during the long, arduous journey—including violence, sexual assault, physical injury, starvation, dehydration, and the loss of family members, to name just a few. In detention centers, migrants may experience separation from family members—including children—and inhumane living conditions. Beatriz, who is from Honduras, talks about her time in various detention centers—she calls each of them a *hielera*, or ice box, because of their deliberate use of cold temperatures—including the Adelanto detention facility, a privately operated immigration detention center in Adelanto, California:

When I entered into the *hielera*, they took everything away from me. My passport, because I had a passport, my cell phone, and now I don't have one. And two officers are coming and the one who [sexually] touched me was like, she's a woman but I don't know what planet she's from, I don't know. She started treating me badly. Do you have lice? She tells me. No, I say. She didn't tell me "take everything off," she took it off from me, and threw them in the trash and degraded me like that, like that, like some kind of animal. I think they treat animals better than us. I go and then she opens my legs and. . . . Everywhere, everywhere, she touched me and I stayed, because I could not call anyone, ask for a call or anything, and she started to say that we are invaders, to insult us. . . . When they brought me down to Adelanto, they took everything from me again and I'm always quiet. And my God, I said, I'm going to die in this confinement and I thought, from here I'm never getting out. I don't know where they are going to take me. . . . Then I started to cry, and began seeing horrible things there. There they treat us badly. They would yell at us. If someone makes a mistake, they punish us all . . . they tell you, "I'll take you to the hole [solitary confinement]." Well, some of them were taken to the hole for eight days, and they came out a little traumatized. One woman came out talking to herself. . . . But the psychological abuse was getting to me, and abuse of the body, I did not feel peace then.

In addition to abuse in detention, upon release they often face racism, xenophobia, and unemployment, along with language, dialect, and culture shock. Any of these traumas can result in depression and anxiety.

Matthew 25 / Mateo 25 is one of the few faith-based organizations we found that included trauma care in their accompaniment model. Others include the United Methodists Welcoming Congregations centers, including the San Gabriel Valley Refugee Children's Center, which we will discuss below, and Fuller Theological Seminary's counseling program, which provides low-cost therapy sessions for asylum seekers referred to by Matthew 25 / Mateo 25 and other organizations.

As of this writing in 2022, twenty-eight asylum seekers had been hosted by seven Matthew 25 / Mateo 25 support circles and another seven hosted by others were provided resources and accompaniment by Matthew 25 / Mateo 25 support circles. Another hundred or so asylum seekers were provided short-term resources and/or referrals to services by Matthew 25 / Mateo 25.

One of the key challenges of the Matthew 25 / Mateo 25 support circle model is recruiting immigrant churches to be a part of partnerships with predominantly white congregations. There are power, cultural, and theological differences that often lead to discomfort among the immigrant congregations working with predominantly white congregations. In terms of power differences, white leaders and laypeople often implicitly assume that things will be done according to their ideas and expectations. According to a Matthew 25 / Mateo 25 leader, "White middle-class or upper-middle-class people get frustrated very quickly with people who see the world differently. I mean some of them are just wonderful human beings, but they center the world around their way of seeing things and people who don't act like that, they push them around. They tell them what to do, they get frustrated, you know, so trying to work together is really, really hard."

Another point of contention is cultural differences in the way organizations should run. White leaders tend to value following organized systems and formal protocols as the proper way to accomplish a task, whereas Latina/o leaders tend to defer to and trust leaders to make decisions and are often willing to work around rules and systems to get things done because often the dominant culture's systems are not designed to work for them. A Latina/o pastor involved in organizing Matthew 25 / Mateo 25 support circles explained these two challenges: "So, the biggest challenge has been getting the [Latino] pastors on board. Again, cultural differences, right. An Anglo pastor handles church differently—they go by the board or there's policies. It's a lot of: 'well, we'll do this but we have to wait for the next board meeting to vote on it.' But when it's like they need something now, we need to do something now. In a Latino church, the pastor has the power." Another Matthew 25 / Mateo 25 leader put the power dynamic this way: "If you want to reach out to Latino pastors to get them involved, they are more engaged in one-on-one, friendly conversations instead of bringing it to them and saying, this is what I want you to do, this is what we have and these are the rules we want you to follow. Pastors usually like to be in control, right?" Another obstacle to recruiting Latina/o pastors to engage in support circles is the time commitment required. "Pastors are busy. Latino pastors are bivocational, they don't have the time or the resources to be full-time pastors so that's been difficult, too because everybody's on the hustle. Like, you want to do ministry but you also got to feed the family. That's been a challenge as well."

Last, theological differences between white and Latina/o congregations have also created obstacles in support circles. The majority of immigrant churches that are most interested in being involved in accompaniment with Matthew 25 / Mateo 25 are evangelical Protestant. Around half of the nonimmigrant congregations in ECAS are evangelical, and the other half are more progressive white mainline congregations, more liberal theologically, which can create tensions. According to one Matthew 25 / Mateo 25 leader:

> Finding churches that would want to walk together in this, but have different theological understandings has also been a challenge. We've tried to connect churches that are similar in their theology, but it's been difficult because a lot of nonimmigrant churches that want to do this work are more liberal in their theology. And there's still a lot of immigrant churches, not just Latino, that are still more conservative. So, there's that

clash. And we present this as, the partnership has nothing to do with [theology]. I mean, theology is important in this because it's a part of Matthew 25 and what Jesus did, but we're going to set our other theological differences aside to be able to focus on this work and I found that that's very difficult for some people.

Matthew 25 / Mateo 25 has tried to bridge the divide between mostly white nonimmigrant congregations and mostly Latina/o immigrant congregations in the support circle by training *puentes*, young, bicultural 1.5-generation Latina/o leaders who act as translators and go-betweens between the two congregations. One of the *puentes* expressed the challenge in negotiating these differences.

As a *puente* you have to navigate who's talking the most, who has the power, it's shared power that we try to go for. For example, in a meeting of a Latino church that doesn't speak English, you have to translate, and you have the white church who's used to doing meetings, who's always used to talking first, you kind of have to slow them down a little more. It's more kind of like power dynamics that I've noticed. It's also the issue of "what we bring." Sometimes the thought is, "Oh, the white church has money so the immigrant has nothing to offer to this." And so, it's kind of building up and reminding the immigrant church that no, you guys have your spirituality, you have your faith, you have your community, you have all these gifts. So, it's more power dynamics and showing each part of the partnership the strengths that they have and how they can bring that to the partnership. I think the other issues are more organizational-wise. With the partnerships, I mean there are going to be pastors who kind of do want to take control, because that's just always how it's going to be. Or take credit. And so, we really try to preach that shared power dynamic. It's hard. You know, a pastor that's been leading a congregation for fifteen to twenty years and has always had the power, and then you tell him like, well, you got to share that. That's not going to work for them. For the Anglo pastors I think it's not like power as in "I want the credit" but it's "I want to run this." Because I'm organized, or I have this degree. In the immigrant church, it's more of "I'm the pastor. I'm the pastor and I don't want to be looked down [upon] by somebody else."

As mentioned above, this innovative structure of combining immigrant and nonimmigrant congregations that are connected by trained *puente* leaders as bridges has a larger goal—of ultimately creating networks of advocacy to advocate for immigration reform. The idea is to unify the church in support of immigrants so that when the opportunity comes again to pass immigration reform, predominantly white nonimmigrant church members will draw from their experience in accompaniment and be more willing to support a more humane and just system. As we have seen, this strategy is supported by empirical research; members of Christian congregations that had programs assisting asylum seekers and refugees were significantly more likely to support the policies of comprehensive immigration reform (Melkonian-Hoover and Kellstedt 2019).

In addition to passing immigration reform, Matthew 25 / Mateo 25 also has the even larger and loftier goal of transforming the church to become a model for the "beloved community" that Dr. Martin Luther King Jr. spoke of, where people of all races and socioeconomic statuses live equally and thrive as brothers and sisters. This ultimate goal requires the transformation of both individuals and the church, and then ultimately the entire society. A Matthew 25 / Mateo 25 leader explains it this way:

> Our goal is the Kingdom of God, our goal is the beloved community. So, it does make sense to put time into changing our opponents. We don't want to defeat them; we want to change them. We want our enemy to join us. It's a different goal. It's also a goal of changing the church. I have this problem with some of our young organizers. They want the low-hanging fruit. We're not just about the low-hanging fruit. We're about the church being the church. Young people tend to want the quickest way to get to an answer. No, we have to work with the people that aren't easy, because that's what makes it work. That makes the bigger goal work. Not just the win but the transformation.

As this leader expressed, the goal of changing individual opponents into allies, changing the church from a divided one to a unified and equal one, and ultimately changing society, is a long-term goal that spans generations, not months or years. This complicated goal requires the investment of time into building relationships between immigrant and nonimmigrant churches that are complicated, are time-consuming, and do not always yield visible measurable results.

While We Care can be seen as a *single-target organization* (Yukich 2013), focusing on accompanying asylum seekers through their asylum cases, Matthew 25 / Mateo 25 is a *multi-target* organization, including accompaniment, education, transforming religious understanding and unifying Christians across racial/ethnic lines, and ultimately advocating for comprehensive immigration reform. Having multiple targets makes strategizing more difficult and time-consuming (Yukich 2013). Matthew 25 / Mateo 25 has evolved more slowly and deliberately in their strategies compared to single-target organizations, whether secular or faith-based, that focus only on accompaniment, advocacy, or other single-target goals. Its goal of pairing immigrant and nonimmigrant congregations to form support circles and thus unify under the common goal of protecting vulnerable immigrants has led to painstaking strategies of meeting together, worshiping together, and training a cadre of *puentes* to translate differences and negotiate conflict. All of this meeting, peacemaking, and strategizing requires an enormous investment of time and emotional energy, which some argue gets in the way of doing the practical work of accompaniment. It has also led some to question whether it would be easier and more efficient to recruit exclusively immigrant congregations to do the work of accompaniment. The complicated and often frustrating nature of combining immigrant and nonimmigrant congregations has led to a turnover of congregations who have cycled in and out of support circles.

However, the leaders of Matthew 25 / Mateo 25 believe that the larger goal of immigration reform will not be possible if white nonimmigrant congregations are not mobilized, since they constitute the bulk of the resistance to immigration reform in the United States. Time will tell whether Matthew 25 / Mateo 25 will succeed in its ultimate goal of influencing policy change by enlisting nonimmigrant churches in the fight for immigration reform, and in the process changing the views of white Christians in the United States toward a more just and welcoming immigration policy. The ambitious long-term goal, however, makes short-term goals more complicated to achieve. Still, the leaders see this long-term goal as central since ultimately there will never be enough resources or people to protect all of those harmed by unjust immigration laws. Simply focusing on the immediate needs of asylum seekers without addressing structural reform is inadequate to their vision of the church unifying to create a more just world.

Place-Based Accompaniment: United Methodist Welcoming Congregations

In addition to flexible networks and support circles, we also saw a third model emerge in our interviews, which we call *place-based accompaniment*. This refers to congregations that by virtue of their location and their facilities and resources were able to provide immigration accompaniment as well as other services to those in their predominantly immigrant neighborhoods. An illustrative example of this is the case of the United Methodist Church's Welcoming Congregations initiative.

In 2014, a surge of unaccompanied minors came to the southern border. In response, the California Pacific Conference of the United Methodist Church (UMC) began an initiative to create four "welcome centers" based in congregations that could serve unaccompanied minors and immigrants. These welcome centers were strategically located in immigrant communities. Through a grant funded by the UMC, they were able to set up centers in their church buildings to provide legal services, mental health care, medical care, spiritual care, and accompaniment for unaccompanied minors and immigrant families in their neighborhoods. They also developed healing therapeutic retreats for unaccompanied minors at a Methodist camp in the mountains called "No Estan Solos" retreats. Key to this strategy is the fact that the Methodist churches in Southern California own large buildings and camps that are underutilized—many were built in the first half of the twentieth century—and once had large memberships but now have small, mostly elderly congregations. Many of these buildings are located in communities that are now home largely to immigrants. The UMC has been intentional about using their buildings and resources to serve the communities around them.

One of the flagship welcoming congregations is North Hills United Methodist Church, which became the site for the San Fernando Valley Refugee Children's Center (SFVRCC). The center operates out of the church building and provides immigration legal services, twice a month group therapy sessions for children and women who have experienced trauma on their immigration journey, and a food and basic needs distribution center that serves families in the neighborhood. In addition to a network of volunteer licensed therapists, SFVRCC also developed a relationship with California State University, Northridge and UCLA, which both provide student interns from their master of social work programs to conduct therapy sessions for minors and families experiencing trauma on their migration journey.

The Methodist model of leveraging their largely empty church buildings is an attractive model for mainline congregations that are property rich but have small congregations. They are reimagining what a church is—a place to care for vulnerable immigrants in their community rather than simply a space for church members to gather for worship on Sunday mornings.

Key to the UMC's place-based strategy is hiring younger immigrant leaders to lead their welcoming congregations' activities. This has been successful in the cases we examined but hasn't been without conflict as this older, theologically progressive, culturally white denomination tries to shift to accommodate young immigrant leaders. According to one young Latino Methodist leader we interviewed, the primary challenge is to make the larger denomination more open and inclusive to younger immigrant leaders of color and less rigid and bureaucratic:

> It's disappointing to see how strong the Methodist church is relying on these institutional boundaries and frameworks that are just becoming less and less relevant. And it's deterring young people of color into ministry or into partnering with Methodist churches. It needs to die to that. Or it needs to reenvision how the Methodist church does that. So, the Methodist church has a great track record of working in a community with great history and great resources and even working with Latinos, but when it comes to institutionalism, like I said it needs to change to accommodate this new era right? What are we really holding onto when it comes to deadlines when it comes to proposals and reports and paperwork. . . . This institutionalism and old structure is not working and that is hindering a lot of the work.

It's a weird [governing] system—it's very democracy-based. So, there are caucuses—these groups I've been in. But at times it's just pointless because all they want is for us to just document it and send a grand proposal and that's it. For Latinos and those that are in the margins it's much more relational; it's a trust building thing. It's not about proposals and deadlines and reports and managing these expectations but it really centers around trusting relationships and molding the work around that. And that's really hard for institutions to do.

Another young Latino Methodist leader also talked at length of the progressive theology of the UMC that often does not translate to Latina/o communities.

And it's even trickier as a Latino Methodist because Methodists have social and political progressivism. Latinos are more progressive-leaning on minimum wage, labor rights, and immigration, but when it comes to family values—all these things they weigh more conservative. There is language coming from white progressives that does not adequately translate into communities of color and there's this assimilation—we have to use this language but I'm of the idea we need to have our own language in house to really express ourselves and what we really represent. And using that [white progressive] language doesn't translate well at all. In Latin America there's not the same idea of left versus right. Those are things that are very different in Latin America and only in the U.S. we Latinos have to deal with the translating of the values of the U.S. American Christianity and making sense of it for the Latino church.

So, while one of the keys to the success of the welcoming congregations model is empowering immigrant leaders to lead the work, the larger denominational structures overseeing the work can lead to cultural clashes and frustration, and according to some, limiting the ability to recruit and retain immigrant leaders.

The UMC, the Catholic Church, and other property-rich denominations have a significant opportunity to retool the use of their significant physical and financial resources for immigrant accompaniment, and the UMC's welcoming congregations model represents a strategy that seems to work effectively. Whether the larger denominations can recruit and retain immigrant leaders to lead these efforts and adapt their formidable denominational structures to new populations seems to be the largest obstacle to expanding this model to more congregations.

The goals of the UMC's Welcoming Congregations initiative are to serve their immigrant communities in whatever capacities are needed, which has come to include legal assistance, trauma care, food provision, youth leadership development, and political organizing for state and local political change. Despite the multiple services offered by this initiative, it is a simpler approach than that of Matthew 25 / Mateo 25 because it exists within a single bureaucracy and is focused on a few particular locations. Like with We Care, the individual welcoming congregations have developed partnerships with other organizations to provide various services and resources, but their goals are more local and limited to serving the populations of their neighborhoods. Their leadership comes completely from within the UMC denomination and therefore is subject to less difficulty in mobilizing a wide array of leaders from multiple traditions. Thus, while the UMC initiative has a wider array of targets than We Care, it is more restricted in its local focus compared to Matthew 25 / Mateo 25. Conflict regarding strategy and organization seems to come primarily from cultural differences within the organization as opposed to between multiple organizations and cultures.

Conclusion: Three Models of Faith-Based Accompaniment

Faith-based organizations are uniquely positioned to provide accompaniment. While more specialized organizations can provide expertise such as legal counsel, trauma care, or education services, faith groups can mobilize volunteers to do the more mundane, but equally important, tasks such as giving people rides, providing food, offering prayer and spiritual support, and in some cases extending a room to stay for months, or even years. The resources that are unique to congregations and faith-based organizations, including large bases of volunteers willing to give time and resources, theologies of justice and caring for others, and a network of people with varied levels of expertise and connections, mean that faith-based organizations are often called upon by other more specialized organizations to take on the bulk of time-consuming labor-intensive accompaniment tasks. Our cases show that coalitions of faith-based organizations doing accompaniment in cooperation with specialized organizations, such as legal aid organizations providing legal services and clinical organizations providing physical and mental health care, are a powerful force for accompanying immigrants.

Another advantage of faith-based accompaniment efforts is that many of the immigrants whom we interviewed have strong religious beliefs and greatly appreciated the spiritual care and connection to faith communities that were provided by faith-based organizations during accompaniment. In fact, a number of those we interviewed claimed that prayer, spiritual support, and friendship were the most important things that they received from others on their migration journey.

We conclude that faith both enables and constrains the ability of faith-based organizations to effectively accompany vulnerable immigrants. Faith-based organizations have the advantage of having access to large numbers of volunteers who are motivated by their faith to do the mundane tasks of caring for people in need. Congregations and faith-based organizations are made up of believers whose faith compels them to open up their homes, give money for food, rent, and bond, give people rides to and from court hearings, watch their children, take people to the store, and listen to and pray for them. Faith-based organizations are uniquely positioned to provide these mundane, yet time-consuming and extremely important, tasks in accompanying vulnerable immigrants.

While secular advocacy organizations typically have staff trained in specific skills such as providing legal aid, job referrals, and strategies for political pressure campaigns, they rarely have access to large numbers of volunteers to care for the basic needs of vulnerable immigrants. Moreover, vulnerable people have not only physical but also spiritual and emotional needs. Having a person care for them, listen to them as they describe their suffering, pray for them, and connect with them on a spiritual level is often as important as the physical needs of someone experiencing the anxieties and trauma of the journey that many migrants experience. Faith-based organizations are uniquely positioned to provide that spiritual and emotional connection.

The constraints that faith creates in doing accompaniment work come from cultural and theological differences that are rooted in the history of religion and colonization in the western hemisphere. The fastest growing religious groups among Latina/o believers are Pentecostal churches, denominations, and organizations, which have been traditionally influenced by Euro-American evangelicalism in their emphasis on individual salvation, traditional family values, and conservative politics. On the other hand, the nonimmigrant religious groups most likely to participate in accompaniment work are more progressive white denominations like the United Methodists. This causes many Latina/o evangelical leaders to be somewhat uncomfortable working with white progressive churches and organizations whose language and political rhetoric are foreign and sometimes offensive to their evangelical subculture, and/or the culture they grew up with in Latin America. For this reason, Matthew 25 / Mateo 25 has sought to connect white evangelical leaders and organizations with their Latina/o brethren in doing accompaniment work together because of their theological affinities, but even this work has been difficult. Cultural and power differences between the two groups create conflicts and obstacles, with white leaders and organizations often taking the lead and expecting to have a strong influence over how the work is done, and having different models of leadership and decision making, while Latina/o leaders are in closer proximity to the people needing accompaniment yet are often left feeling disrespected and ignored. Even when faith-based organizations are committed to centering immigrant leadership, these obstacles are difficult to overcome, and therefore long-lasting partnerships between immigrant-led and nonimmigrant-led organizations are rare.

Last, we saw a clear distinction between "single-target" and "multi-target" (Yukich 2013) organizations. Both have their advantages and constraints. Matthew 25 / Mateo 25, for example, is a multi-target organization that has not only the narrow goal of meeting the immediate needs of vulnerable immigrants but also the larger goals of passing comprehensive immigration reform and transforming the politically and racially divided Christian community in the United States into a unified "beloved community." We witnessed how these multiple goals often conflict with each other and make the work of accompaniment more difficult. Single-target organizations, like the Latina/o-immigrant-led We Care, are much narrower in their focus on meeting the immediate needs of asylum seekers and advocating for their legal residency status. However, as effective as organizations like We Care are in helping large numbers of individuals, as noted earlier, without comprehensive immigration reform, there will never be enough volunteers to meet the needs of and obtain legal residency for the millions of people harmed by the U.S. immigration system. Thus, a strategy of "converting" anti-immigrant white Christians to the cause of immigration reform appears to be a fraught but necessary project.

4

Advocacy

In the 1980s, Luis Reyes was kidnapped as a young child in Guatemala by an armed guerrilla group during the civil war.[1] His family thought that he had been killed and fled to the United States for safety. After five years Luis somehow escaped from his captors and went searching for his family, miraculously found them, and at the age of thirteen crossed the U.S. border without authorization to join his family. In 1993 at the age of eighteen, Clinton administration officials deported him back to Guatemala. He crossed the border without authorization again soon after to rejoin his family and has been in the United States ever since. In 2003, Luis married his high school sweetheart Jenny, a U.S. citizen whom he had met at church. They now have two children in elementary school, both U.S. citizens. Luis explains his immigration situation:

> When I was a teenager, immigration grabbed me, and I had deportation orders, and we always tried under other administrations to fix our documents, but they always told us that we had to leave the country for ten years. When I got married, how am I going to leave my wife? When the children came, I thought how can I leave my children? We were all trusting in God since we heard rumors that it was very likely that there would be immigration reform, so we clung to hope and cried out to God to ask God that this would be possible. I have never had any criminal record, thanks to God, I did not commit any crime in this nation. The only crime, if it can be called that, has been that I have crossed the border undocumented.

Pastor Luis became an evangelical Christian in 1992 at age seventeen and began attending a small Latina/o immigrant evangelical church in Los Angeles with members from all over Mexico and Central and South America. He remained a member of that church for more than twenty years before becoming a pastor and starting his own congregation, which began meeting in his home and is affiliated with the Assemblies of God denomination. His church is now a small but thriving congregation that meets in a strip mall in Los Angeles. He is also a contractor and owns a small construction business that has a number of employees.

In 2015, with little hope for immigration reform on the horizon, Pastor Luis felt that God was wanting him to make his immigration situation right. So the Reyes family contacted an attorney. According to Luis,

> This lawyer took my case under the Obama administration. She told me, "You owe nothing to anyone, you have no criminal record, you are a good person, you are a pastor." She took me there to the immigration office and she did everything that had to be done and thanks to God she was able to get a stay of deportation. And through that she got me a work permit. We just had to check in every year to renew the stay of deportation. But suddenly in 2017 she received a call, because President Trump came in. She said, "We don't know what will happen now. You are a priority for deportation now, even if you have not committed crimes or anything." And that put me in tremendous anguish.

Under the Obama administration, undocumented immigrants like Pastor Luis who had not committed any crimes and who had spouses and children who were U.S. citizens were not prioritized for deportation and were given stays of removal—which means as long as they checked in once a year with ICE to ensure they had not committed any crimes, they would not be targeted for deportation. However, within days of the inauguration of President Trump, the administration eliminated this system of prioritization, blocked stays of deportation, and directed ICE officers to take enforcement action "against all removable aliens" (Executive Order 13768, 2017). Pastor Luis's lawyer informed him that there was now a high probability that he would be detained at his next ICE check-in.

As a result, he contacted Pastor Ada Valiente, the cofounder of We Care. Ada and the leaders of Matthew 25 / Mateo 25 mobilized a network of pastors, denominations, and faith-based organizations to advocate for Pastor Luis in an attempt to keep him from getting detained. Meetings were held between faith leaders and ICE officials to inform them about Luis's situation and to ask them for another stay of deportation. In these meetings, some ICE officials admitted that people like Pastor Luis—noncitizens with no criminal record, business owners, pastors, fathers with citizen families—were not those whom they wanted to prioritize for deportation. But they explained that they were under the command of the Department of Homeland Security (DHS) and they had to comply with directives coming from Washington.

In April 2017, Pastor Luis was scheduled to have his annual ICE check-in. Around thirty faith leaders, advocates, and supporters held a prayer vigil and press conference outside of ICE headquarters in downtown Los Angeles to pray that he would not be detained and that his stay of removal would be approved for another year. Several faith leaders accompanied him to his meeting with ICE officials. He was not detained at that time but was told by ICE officials to come back in three months. Another large prayer vigil and press conference was held at ICE headquarters and faith leaders again accompanied him to his July 2017 check-in. Pastor Luis describes that day:

> I came back in July of 2017 and I will never forget this, because we were down there, there were many organizations that accompanied us, many people. And among them were also my wife and my children, my daughter and my son. And my daughter says to me, "Daddy, are you going to take too long up there?" And I said to her—"No, no *mija*, this is going to be fast right now. I'm going to go downstairs and we're going to have breakfast at Denny's." And she was very happy and everything, but I never came back out. They detained me and the officers moved me so fast from there. I had heard of the Adelanto detention center, but I never knew what it was. In a matter of hours, they transported me quickly to the Adelanto detention center, a terrible place, a horrible place—I think there should not be places like the Adelanto detention center.

Pastor Luis went on to describe his experience at Adelanto, a for-profit immigration detention facility owned and operated by the GEO corporation in the high desert eighty-five miles northeast of downtown Los Angeles:

> It was a terrible experience. There you suffer humiliations of the worst kind. There they humiliate you terribly, a terrible psychological torture

that is suffered in that place. But the saddest, the most painful, the strongest, greatest suffering that can be experienced in that place, is the separation from the family. There is no greater suffering for a human being than the suffering of separation from the family. It took over three weeks before they could visit me there. They gave us permission to hug at first but my children kept watching me and they tried to touch me and the officer shouted that they could not touch me. So, I looked at them, and they thought that maybe their dad doesn't want to hug them, he doesn't want to cuddle them as he was always used to, and they didn't know that their father was dying, coming undone inside to not be able to hug them. It was a terrible thing that I would not wish on anyone.

In addition to the daily humiliations and emotional distress of being apart from his family, Pastor Luis became ill with bronchitis while in detention. Despite repeated attempts to get medical treatment for his bronchitis, he was refused until it turned into pneumonia, putting his life at risk, at which point he finally received medical care. A 2019 DHS Inspector General report confirmed accounts of expired food, unhealthy conditions, and inadequate medical care at Adelanto (DHS 2019b). Formerly detained individuals whom we interviewed claim that the daily verbal humiliations, poor-quality food, hot and cold temperatures, and refusal of medical care inside Adelanto represent a not-so-subtle attempt to get detainees to sign deportation waivers that would allow ICE to immediately deport them without going through the official hearings needed to finalize deportation orders.

After Pastor Luis's detention, the network of Southern California faith leaders and organizations that tried to prevent his detention mobilized to advocate for his release. The key organizations leading this effort were Matthew 25 / Mateo 25, LARED (Liberation. Action. Respect. Equity. Dignity), COPALA (La Coalicion de Pastores Latinos de Los Angeles), CLUE, LA Voice, We Care, and the Assemblies of God denomination of which Pastor Luis's congregation is a part. They employed both "grasstops" (influential faith leaders connecting directly to decision makers in government) and "grassroots" (mobilizing congregation members to attend rallies, send letters, and make phone calls to decision makers) strategies.

During this campaign, numerous prayer vigils to "Free Pastor Luis" at ICE headquarters in downtown Los Angeles were led by Latina/o-led faith-based organizations and covered by local and national media, including the *Los Angeles Times*, CNN, CBS, Telemundo, Univision, the *Nation*, and Buzzfeed. His case was covered in national evangelical Christian publications as well, including *Christianity Today*, the *Christian Post*, and *Sojourners*. Influential faith leaders held meetings with ICE and DHS officials regarding his case. Eight Latina/o national leaders within the Assemblies of God denomination approached George Wood, the head of the denomination at the time, to use his connections to President Trump to advocate for Pastor Luis's release directly to the president, which he did.

Matthew 25 / Mateo 25 also mobilized a written letter and email prayer campaign directed toward the ICE officials who had jurisdiction over Luis's case. Hundreds of individuals sent email prayers to one official respectfully telling him that they were praying for him in his difficult job and that God would give him the ability to make good and just decisions regarding the immigration cases he had jurisdiction over, including Pastor Luis's. More than a dozen churches had their members, including children, write letters to this particular official telling him they were praying for him. Leaders in the Catholic Church also approached him to advocate on behalf of Pastor Luis.

After two months, none of this advocacy campaign seemed to be working. Pastor Luis was ready to surrender hope and prepare to be deported. The ICE officials at Adelanto kept telling him he was definitely going to be deported and that there was no hope for him. They told him it would happen soon. He vividly describes a moment when he gave up hope:

> The night before, I had poured out my soul, like water at the feet of Christ, and I said to the Lord that I couldn't take it anymore. I realized that I had been lying there on the floor for more than three hours, and I had said—"I can't stand this anymore." That night my wife was going to visit me because that was my daughter's birthday. I said to my wife, "Stay home. I don't think our daughter wants to see me." She said, "I want to give you a hug." "No, stay there," I said. Well, they left and the car broke down on the freeway. The children were crying desperately in the car just at that moment when I called her, and I heard my son, the youngest little boy crying, uncontrollably, and one of the things he said was, "Dad, you

are my hero and you told me that you were never going to abandon us," because I always told him this, that we are always going to be together, and now is the time the child needs you most when they are talking like this. "Now when I need you the most, where are you? Why are you not with us?" The boy is crying and he is inconsolable, when all that happened to them on the freeway, and at that moment it was something terrible, at that moment they cut off my call—the officers of Adelanto cut my communication. At that time I called a cousin and he contacted my wife and later Pastor Valiente went to pick up my wife where the car broke down and it was a tremendous situation. So that night, I threw myself down and said to God—I can't take it anymore. I said—I can't take this anymore, it's too much for me, look how my children are suffering, look how my wife is suffering. Look how the church is suffering—and I said to him—I can't stand it anymore—and in that moment that I'm there, I suddenly felt that he put a hand on my head. But something supernatural like I had never experienced, and a peace began to enter me, that peace that passes all understanding, that cannot be understood, cannot be explained. And at the end of all that I was defeated and I said to the Lord these words, I said, "God, if this is what you want for me, if you want me to continue in this place, or if you want me to be deported, and keep giving your word, take your word to other places, here I am sir, here I am. And do to me what is good. And if it seems better here to you, here I am, I just beg you please, do not forget my wife, and my children, and the church. Look at my children, how are they? I only ask you to hug them, to console them, to strengthen them," and after saying that, I got up. Right, I got up. Very happy, a different man, looking at things differently.

The very next morning, Pastor Luis got the news that he was being released. "They told me after eight in the morning that at twelve o'clock noon they were going to give me some news and at twelve they called me in there. And then they said—prepare your things because you are going home and when he said that, oh, [other detainees] at that moment came. They hugged me and we started crying with joy, because I was going to leave, but others were crying with sadness because I was going to leave." That day, Pastor Ada Valiente had taken Jenny Reyes and her kids to Disneyland to celebrate the Reyes daughter's birthday. That night, as they were leaving Disneyland they received a call from Pastor Luis's lawyer that he was being released. They all broke down in tears and could not believe that this had happened.

After over two months in detention, Pastor Luis was allowed to reunite with his family. His immigration case, however, as of this writing in 2022, is still unresolved. He is still required to check in with ICE every three months. His deportation order was not rescinded, but he was told that he could reopen his case and that he will not be deported while his case is being processed. There are no guarantees from ICE, however, that he will not be detained again and eventually deported. The Biden administration is not currently prioritizing people like him for deportation. But the fact that his case is still unresolved causes much stress and anxiety for him and his family. Jenny explains the psychological toll that all of this has taken on her and their children: "It was like losing my husband so it's like I was in mourning also. I would talk to him but it wasn't the same as having that person physically by your side. So, it was very hard and being here at the house alone with my children and taking them to school."

She and her children continue to suffer from anxiety, and the children fear that their parents will be taken away.

> I have to see a therapist and I'm currently taking my medication because my anxiety level was so high so I'm under medication right now. But it's like a taboo. You can't talk to anybody about it. It's been pretty hard on my children. My son suffers a lot from anxiety and my daughter too. They're just scared all the time. My son is scared all the time. My daughter, she worries a lot and she gets really bad stomach cramps. And that's how it is. So, I have to assure them all the time. When I go to the doctor they're scared. They're crying. They say that they're scared that I'm not going to come back or something.

It is difficult to say what made the difference in this advocacy campaign to get pastor Luis released. It seems clear, however, that without the nationwide advocacy campaign Pastor Luis, like many others in his situation, would have been deported and separated from his family indefinitely.

A number of faith leaders we interviewed from numerous organizations cited Pastor Luis's release from detention as one of the most encouraging victories of their advocacy work. Not only was Pastor Luis's release secured and he was allowed to continue his appeal for legal residency, but the case received national media coverage and illustrated the cruelty and arbitrary nature of the enforcement policies and priorities of the Trump administration. It also created sympathy, especially among Christians across the political spectrum, for resisting policies that separated families and that detained and deported fellow Christians who by all measures are positive contributors to their communities. Another win that came from Pastor Luis's campaign was that the General Council of the Assemblies of God denomination (the national leadership office) agreed to allow official credentials to be given to undocumented pastors, something that they had never done before. The national leadership of the denomination saw the impact and value of Pastor Luis's ministry and decided to make this change in policy going forward.

Defining Advocacy

A common definition of advocacy is mobilizing for policy change, whether at the national, state, or local level. In this book we expand our definition of advocacy to include advocacy for individual immigration cases and class-action lawsuits. During the Trump administration immigration policy change came not from federal immigration law revisions but rather from executive orders changing priorities and tactics in immigration enforcement. Therefore, while faith leaders and organizations continued to advocate for comprehensive immigration reform, the lion's share of energy and mobilization went toward resisting the new protocols for enforcement carried out by CBP and ICE, which included highlighting cases like Pastor Luis's. As one faith-based organizer told us, "We are on defense right now, not offense."

The Faith-Based Advocacy Response

The changes in immigration enforcement policy implemented by the Trump administration led to massive increases in detention, family separation, and abuse of immigrants (Pierce and Bolter 2020). Faith leaders and organizations responded through advocacy by using three basic strategies: (1) direct lobbying, (2) class-action lawsuits, and (3) advocacy for state and local policy change. Since the Trump administration's policy changes were changes not in immigration law but in enforcement through executive actions, it was difficult to resist them through policy advocacy. As a result, most faith leaders and organizations chose to focus on direct lobbying for individual cases and changes in enforcement practices. The exception was advocacy for the end to the zero-tolerance policy that separated children from their parents at the border. A nationwide outcry, including from faith leaders, like Franklin Graham, who otherwise supported President Trump's immigration policies, as well as federal lawsuits eventually discontinued this practice. Some success was also achieved through class-action lawsuits as well as advocacy for changes in state and local laws, and in both cases faith-based and secular organizations joined forces to mobilize. With the Biden administration in place, these organizations began again advocating for federal legislative reform, although many of the enforcement protocols introduced during the Trump administration remained in place, including the controversial Title 42 and "remain in Mexico" orders that force asylum seekers to wait in Mexico while their claims are processed. The three main strategies used by faith leaders for these three types of advocacy emphasized during the Trump administration are explained and illustrated below.

Direct Lobbying: Matthew 25 / Mateo 25

The case of Pastor Luis Reyes illustrates a strategy of the direct lobbying of decision makers by faith leaders and organizations. Pastor Luis's case was chosen by faith leaders because it (1) included a faith leader with whom many people of faith, including evangelicals, would sympathize; (2) was egregious in its injustice, targeting an individual who had no criminal record, who had been in the United States for decades, and who had a family of U.S. citizens; and (3) included a pastor and business owner in his community. Because of these ingredients, faith-based organizers reasoned that pastor Luis's case would be likely to receive national attention and would highlight the injustices of the new enforcement priorities. In addition, some of these leaders knew his family personally and as a result deeply cared about the outcome of his case. The organizations involved used both grasstops and grassroots strategies to directly lobby government officials at the local and national levels who had the ability to release pastor Luis. The direct lobbying had a distinctively faith-based approach. For example, individual letters to ICE officials on behalf of Pastor Luis were framed as prayers for the ICE official. We heard anecdotal evidence that these officials were affected by those letters and prayers.

During the Trump administration, Matthew 25 / Mateo 25, in cooperation with other leaders and organizations, was involved in a number of direct lobbying efforts that illustrate the unique resources of faith-based organizations to lobby decision makers. One of the cases of direct lobbying included pressuring Homeland Security director Chad Wolf to release detained immigrants who were vulnerable to COVID-19 once it became clear that the virus was spreading in immigration facilities. A leader of Matthew 25 / Mateo 25 explains how their leaders, along with other leaders of a group called Christian Churches Together (CCT), lobbied Wolf to commit to releasing COVID-19-vulnerable people from detention:

> CCT was a place where evangelicals and people from the World Council of Churches and Catholics and Orthodox could all come together so that there could continue to be dialogue and joint work. It has always played this important quiet role of bringing together people across these lines. So when Carlos Malave became director of CCT a few years ago, he decided to get Hispanic leaders of these denominations together. It didn't really take off until about a year ago when COVID-19 started. So he had people from Foursquare, Assemblies of God, Apostolic, and Church of God and Methodists, Lutherans, and Catholics. So he called together all of the Hispanic leaders to pray about COVID-19. And he had a series of prayer sessions. But you know Matthew 25—we always come with action in mind. I always show up at those meetings thinking what can we do, right? There are other people that are part of it that think that way too. In the beginning it was all denominational folks that don't think that way really, we're just praying together. Which was great, particularly in the Hispanic community it created relationships. But basically, we said to folks, "What can we do?" At that moment it was clear that people were going to die. They had just made this decision on a national level that they would be willing to release people from prison, but not from immigration detention.

Chad Wolf made that a public statement. So that statement came out, and then we wrote a letter immediately, I mean literally within twenty-four hours and we had a bunch of the leaders from CCT sign it—twenty-five of them. But they signed it as representing their denominations. But we didn't just send it. We knew if we just sent it, it wouldn't mean anything. So, we went two different directions at once. One is that World Relief [an arm of the National Association of Evangelicals] was willing to take it on our behalf to Chad Wolf. And then wherever we were located around the country everyone agreed that they would take it to their legislators. So, it came to Chad Wolf from two directions. It came from the top, and of course World Relief is part of the National Association of Evangelicals, and then it came from people going to their legislators and then the legislators contacted Chad Wolf. And then the day after the letter was sent, he announced that they would start letting people in immigration detention go as well. At that point everybody jumped on, the whole universe, all of the interfaith immigration coalitions, everybody wrote letters. But it turned out that that whole big push turned out to be necessary, and not only that but the lawsuits also, because it's one thing for him to announce that but it's another thing to have it actually happen.

This case is instructive for several reasons. First, it shows that networks of high-level faith leaders can gain access to high-level decision makers and policy makers quickly if they work together. Second, it shows that it takes a catalyst with organizing experience, such as the Matthew 25 / Mateo 25 leader above, to mobilize the network. Third, while Wolf made a public commitment to release COVID-19-vulnerable immigrant detainees as a result of this "grasstops" pressure from religious leaders, very few detainees were actually released until "grassroots" forces were mobilized and class-action lawsuits were filed to pressure ICE to comply with Wolf's order. According to the Matthew 25 / Mateo 25 leader quoted above, in faith-based direct lobbying, "Successful organizing, in my experience, is always a mixture of grassroots and grasstops."

The example above illustrates the power of influential religious leaders to pressure public officials to act. However, there is a deeper level of direct lobbying that involves building close relationships with decision makers who share the same faith commitments and in which faith leaders see themselves as "ministering to" or "discipling" public officials to act in ways consistent with their common faith. This type of lobbying requires not only access to officials but also the ability to form long-term relationships and connect with them on a deep level, relationally and spiritually. Matthew 25 / Mateo 25 leaders specialize in this latter form of direct lobbying. According to one Matthew 25 / Mateo 25 leader,

> Our advocacy is different. It's not just advocacy. It's not enough to just join the secular folks. We do that too, but we also bring our unique gifts. Those are pastoral conversations. They are different. We have pastoral conversations with people from ICE. We have pastoral conversations with key legislators. We come in to disciple them because these are people with a faith commitment. . . . Government officials are supposed to meet with the community but they would much rather meet with us than with the immigrant rights groups. For some of them we are their way of meeting with the community. Because we do it the way that we do it. When we meet with officials in the government that are people of faith, it's a very different quality of discussion. We talk to them about their faith. We talk about "What is God calling us to do? What is God calling you to do?" So, they are very deep conversations. That's why they don't want people knowing about our meetings. They get really vulnerable and talk about what it's like personally, to make these decisions. Successful organizing is always a combination of hard confrontation and deeply human negotiation. All of that has to be part of the mix. And often the part of it that is deeply human encounter, the deeply spiritual encounter happens quietly. It's not public because if it's public, you lose all of the power. It's an intimate interaction. Frederick Douglass said that power never gives up power without a struggle. But what he didn't say is sometimes that struggle is happening within the powerful person. You can become an ally, especially if they are a believer, of the part of them that wants something more—that wants what God wants, that wants the common good. But that work is intimate work.

Matthew 25 / Mateo 25, because they mobilize evangelicals, have access to conservative and Republican leaders that other groups do not have access to. In one successful direct lobbying effort organized by Matthew 25 / Mateo 25, prominent local evangelical pastors from one immigrant and one nonimmigrant congregation met with Mimi Walters, then an

Orange County Republican House representative and a person of faith, to encourage her to sign on to an effort in the House to protect DACA. In the end she was one of only six California Republican House members to support the effort.

Another direct lobbying effort in which Matthew 25 / Mateo 25 leaders participated was with key officials that resulted in several individual immigrant cases being resolved. The leaders we interviewed, however, did not want to speak about the details of this effort because it involved faith leaders meeting with high-level officials on a regular basis and sharing deeply about the spiritual aspects of the decisions that these officials make, and these public officials do not want these meetings to be made public.

A Matthew 25 / Mateo 25 leader explained the difference between the direct lobbying work that they do and that of secular immigrant rights organizations:

> We bring different gifts to the table. And those different gifts are connected to different goals. Secular groups, they are focused on the next win. We are focused on a deeper transformation. They wouldn't take the time to set up these regular meetings with officials. Because it would be a detour. They are focused on the next win, the next fight. But secular groups would agree that if you could build a deeper movement that transformed your enemies to neutral and your neutral to allies, you should do it. Which is why they work with us because they see that we bring that. But they don't have much of an interest in doing that. Brilliant organizing is both short and long term. But faith organizing by necessity is long term. Our goal is different. Our goal is the Kingdom of God, our goal is the beloved community.

This quote illustrates a unique aspect of faith-based organizing. Faith leaders are willing to pursue long-term goals that require time-consuming relationship building with officials because of their faith—no effort is wasted when it comes to pursuing the Kingdom of God. This motivates the faithful to keep pursuing the goal when it looks hopeless or when time-consuming activities seem futile. They are convinced that God is behind their efforts and that eventually this beloved community will come into being.

While Pastor Luis's case and other individual cases were resolved through direct lobbying like those described above, there were also a few examples where direct lobbying affected enforcement policy at a national level. One was the example of COVID-19-vulnerable detainees being released, and another was the effort to reunify families separated by the zero-tolerance policy. While these enforcement changes can be seen as successes, attempts to change immigration enforcement policy were largely unsuccessful because of Trump's commitment to make good on his campaign promise to crack down on immigration and to mobilize support among his base of white evangelical anti-immigrant voters. The realization early on among faith leaders committed to immigration reform that policy change was unlikely during the Trump administration led to their advocacy mostly toward freeing individuals from detention and preventing their deportation.

The primary strategy that faith-based organizations used to advocate for individuals has been providing legal services and money for bond. A 2016 study found that only 14 percent of detained immigrants had access to legal counsel and that those who did were four times more likely to be released from detention (44 vs. 11 percent) and more than seventeen times more likely to successfully challenge their deportation (17 vs. less than 1 percent) (Eagly and Shafer 2016). Faith-based organizations such as CLUE, We Care, Catholic Charities, and United Methodist Welcoming Congregations collaborate with secular nonprofits such as Al Otro Lado, CHIRLA, RAICES, the ACLU, and many other organizations to provide individuals with legal representation and money to bond out of detention. This strategy has had a high success rate of getting detainees released from detention while their cases are being processed. As noted earlier, We Care claims that almost all of the people for whom they have secured legal assistance have been released from detention while their cases were being processed. It is difficult to say, however, the success rate of these cases resulting in stays of deportation or legal residency.

Civil Suit Advocacy: CLUE

Faith-based organizations also joined class-action lawsuits as witnesses to make the case that Trump's immigration enforcement policies were unconstitutional. This strategy included partnerships between faith-based organizations and legal advocacy groups joining together to sue federal government agencies and their contractors in court.

An organization that illustrates this strategy is CLUE, a Los Angeles–based interfaith advocacy organization. CLUE is involved in a number of campaigns regarding immigration reform and has a full-time organizer, Guillermo Torres, to direct their efforts in immigration advocacy.

CLUE was one of the organizations involved in the campaign described above to release Pastor Luis Reyes. During this campaign Torres was struck by the abusive treatment that detainees received at Adelanto detention facility. Soon after Pastor Luis was released a group of nine detainees went on a hunger strike to protest the abusive conditions at Adelanto. CLUE joined with other organizations to publicize the hunger strike and the abuse that the hunger strikers received in retaliation for their strike. As a result of the media attention, a number of civil rights organizations joined a class-action lawsuit to sue the GEO corporation that owns and runs the detention facility and ICE for the abusive treatment of the hunger strikers. According to Torres,

> [The hunger strikers] were physically assaulted, pepper sprayed, not only in their face but in their private parts, and they were thrown in hot showers so that the pepper spray would burn more. It was horrible, they were beat up. . . . We did a lot of media advocacy to spread the word of what was happening inside those detention centers; bringing this issue to people's conscience and then we did a campaign to get [the hunger strikers] all out by having our congregations cooperate to bond them out and to also sponsor housing for them. Then, we helped initiate a civil rights lawsuit with one of our close friends who is a civil rights attorney and she along with two other attorneys filed a civil rights lawsuit against GEO and ICE to seek damages for the harm they caused the hunger strikers. So, the advocacy was done through working with partner attorneys, civil rights attorneys, and working with a coalition of other organizations.

As a result of this advocacy, the hunger strikers were released from detention and GEO settled with them for an undisclosed sum.

After this initial lawsuit, CLUE joined a partnership with Freedom for Immigrants, a nonprofit organization that had created a national visitation network where trained volunteers meet regularly with inmates at immigration detention facilities around the country, listen to them, pray with them, care for them, and document human rights abuses at the facility; that documentation can then be used in civil lawsuits and advocacy campaigns. Torres mobilized congregations in CLUE's Southern California network to recruit volunteers to visit detainees at Adelanto and document human rights violations. Torres explains it this way: "We created trainings for people to visit immigrants in detention. That's very important because they can understand their pain and suffering and they can find out from them directly what they are going through in the detention centers. So that creates a kind of witness program where people now become witnesses and can share this information with the outside world. In some cases, they will start sharing this with their representatives, their government officials about these conditions." In addition to using this information in lawsuits and advocacy campaigns, these witnesses also share about the abusive conditions and human rights violations with their congregations.

> This group was very powerful because when we started that program for visiting immigrants in detention about three years ago many people did not know, they did not ever connect to an immigrant or visit someone in detention. So, they became witnesses to other people to tell them what they saw, what they heard, and what the abuses are that were going on there. Some of the attorneys don't have access to their clients because sometimes Adelanto locks people down and they don't give them access to their attorneys. We are kind of the eyes on the ground there, that is one of the roles of the faith communities that we are able get that information and get it out to legal agencies, media, and partners so that they can use it for their advocacy and for the legal litigations.

Freedom for Immigrants created a database that documented abuses and human rights violations in detention centers around the nation. One of CLUE's volunteers eventually became the database manager. The database is used in media advocacy campaigns and lawsuits to highlight the abusive conditions in immigration detention.

As a result of this witness program initiated by CLUE, Freedom for Immigrants, and the Inland Coalition for Immigrant Justice (another faith-based organization), a federal class-action lawsuit was filed (*Frai-*

hat v. ICE) that represented the class of approximately fifty-five thousand immigrants detained around the nation by ICE. The suit challenged ICE for not providing adequate medical care and mental health care for detainees, for using solitary confinement as a punishment in ways that violated the due process clause of the Fifth Amendment, and for not making adequate accommodations for detainees with disabilities. The suit was filed by a coalition of legal aid nonprofits, including the Civil Rights Education and Enforcement Center (CREEC), Disability Rights Advocates (DRA), and the Southern Poverty Law Center (SPLC). CLUE and Freedom for Immigrants filed an amicus brief in this case documenting abuses at Adelanto.

While the *Fraihat* case was being litigated, the COVID-19 pandemic broke out, putting vulnerable detainees at risk of dying due to outbreaks in detention facilities. The initiators of the *Fraihat* case (CREEC, DRA, and SPLC) filed a motion for a preliminary injunction to stop ICE from detaining immigrants and to release medically vulnerable detainees if the agency would not take further action to prevent the spread of COVID-19. In addition, another class-action lawsuit was filed by the ACLU (*Roman v. Wolf*) to drastically reduce the number of detainees at Adelanto in order to allow for social distancing inside of the facility and to protect vulnerable detainees from being infected with the virus. As a result of the ACLU suit, in April 2020 a federal judge ordered Adelanto to immediately stop accepting new detainees and to reduce the detainee population to such a level that would allow the remaining detainees to maintain a social distance of six feet from each other at all times and at all places.

The DHS appealed the *Roman* decision and successfully fought for a stay of implementing the order to reduce the population while the case was being heard at the Ninth District Court of Appeals. By September 2020 there were fifty-eight confirmed cases of COVID-19 at Adelanto and evidence, according to the ACLU, that ICE was secretly refusing to test all of the detainees in order to hide the extent of the outbreak.

During the week of October 12, 2020, CLUE organized a weeklong hunger strike at ICE headquarters in downtown Los Angeles to advocate for the release of COVID-19-vulnerable detainees at Adelanto and highlighted two COVID-19-vulnerable undocumented Latino evangelical pastors detained at Adelanto. Tents were set up on the sidewalk outside of the building where strikers camped out for the week. The strike included family members of the two detained pastors and their support-ers. Numerous church groups came during the week to pray with the strikers for the release of vulnerable detainees, to lead worship music and singing, and to give emotional support to the strikers.

On October 15, three days into the hunger strike, the Ninth District Court ruled in favor of the plaintiffs and ordered Adelanto to release detainees vulnerable to COVID-19 and to reduce its detainee population to a level that made social distancing possible. This led to the release of over two hundred fifty detainees from Adelanto.

In these successful lawsuits, CLUE and Freedom for Immigrants pro-vided key evidence of medical neglect and mistreatment, including the use of the dangerous chemical HDQ, which was being spread inside the facility in an attempt to contain the outbreak and led to health problems among inmates, including lung damage, breathing problems, and head-aches. According to Torres,

> We were a part of the brief before the ACLU [*Roman v. Wolf*] lawsuit. We were a part of the *Fraihat* case which was the groundwork for the ACLU lawsuit that came after. We actually were a sign on to the lawsuit as an organization. Then as a part of the coalition with our partners, we worked together with them and other organizations this year to amplify the issue of the spraying of the chemicals. We had Univision do a three-part inves-tigative story about the chemicals. We had a key role in that because we constantly meet with the detainees. They let us know what the conditions are there or what is happening there. We are able to use that information both as declarations to be able to reach out to the media and do advocacy.

In addition to providing media attention and key evidence of mistreat-ment at Adelanto for the class-action lawsuits, CLUE coordinated with six churches in the Los Angeles area that were shut down because of the COVID-19 pandemic to temporarily house some of the two hundred fifty released detainees from Adelanto in their unused church buildings while they looked for long-term housing. Other congregations and vol-unteers mobilized by CLUE provided beds, food, and supplies for their temporary stay at these churches.

CLUE's collaboration with other organizations to combine accompa-niment of detained and released vulnerable immigrants and advocacy through class-action lawsuits and public demonstrations is a strategic response to advocacy in a political environment where legislative change is not realistic. This case shows that congregations full of people who are willing to personally care for vulnerable and suffering people can be mobilized for effective advocacy.

Local and State Policy Advocacy: LA Voice

Because the national political environment was hostile toward reforming federal immigration laws, faith-based activists in Southern California began to focus on state and local policy toward immigration enforcement. While border management and immigration law are federal issues, state and local laws determine the relationship between ICE and local law enforcement. Local police and sheriff's departments often cooperate with ICE in sharing information and allowing access to undocumented immigrants in local and state courts, jails, and prisons. This relationship between ICE and local law enforcement became a key focus for immigrant advocacy groups in Southern California during the Trump administration.

Faith-based advocacy groups in Southern California mobilized around the so-called Sanctuary State bill (California SB54), which sought to limit cooperation between local law enforcement agencies and ICE. SB54 was passed in October 2017 and went into effect on January 1, 2018. Among other things, it prohibits law enforcement from asking someone about their immigration status or detaining them solely because of their status or assisting ICE in detaining individuals released from jail or prison. The faith community advocating for immigrants thought this was an important bill to rally behind because it not only protects people from being detained by police for immigration violations but also makes immigrant communities more willing to call the police if they are victims or witnesses of crime without the fear of having their immigration status scrutinized.

Jeff Sessions, U.S. attorney general at the time, responded to the bill's passage by filing a lawsuit in federal court insisting that California was unconstitutionally interfering with federal immigration enforcement. More than a dozen local governments in Southern California either joined the Jeff Sessions lawsuit or made public statements supporting it, including the Orange County Board of Supervisors. Faith groups such as Matthew 25 / Mateo 25, CLUE, LA Voice, and Solidarity, in conjunction with secular immigrant rights groups, organized to have community members show up at city council meetings all over Los Angeles and Orange counties urging their council members and mayors during public comments to refrain from joining the Sessions lawsuit.

On April 3, 2018, in the Orange County city of Fullerton, 103 members of the community spoke up to address the city council's deliberation on whether or not to join the Sessions lawsuit—the community comments session lasted over six hours (La Tour 2018). Faith-based nonprofits, including Solidarity and Matthew 25 / Mateo 25, joined with secular immigrant rights nonprofits such as the Korean Resource Center to speak in opposition to the lawsuit. Of the 103 who spoke at the meeting, 98 argued against the Sessions lawsuit and approximately half cited their faith as the reason why they opposed the lawsuit. Many read Bible verses stating that God calls on his people to welcome immigrants. These faith-infused speeches were designed by the faith-based organizers to appeal to the Christian faith of certain members of the city council who were undecided on the issue. One of the council members, a person of faith, changed their vote that night, resulting in a narrow decision not to join the suit.

LA Voice is a faith-based organization that was highly engaged in the campaign to pass SB54. The group is part of a national network of faith-based organizers called Faith in Action. The model of organizing that LA Voice uses is to recruit congregations to participate in grassroots campaigns for justice. Once a congregation signs on, the congregation creates a local organizing committee (LOC) and is assigned a full-time organizer from LA Voice, whose organizers then meet with congregational LOCs regularly; the LOCs set the agenda of what campaigns they would like to join, which are typically issues of local or state government policy. LA Voice then connects LOCs with ongoing campaigns in progress and trains them in grassroots tools to mobilize their congregations, such as phone banking, public actions, visiting legislators, and letter writing. LA Voice has approximately sixty congregations in Los Angeles County in its network and seven full-time organizers to mobilize them. Marvin Andrade, lead organizer at LA Voice, explains the organizing strategy and structure this way:

Every LA Voice organizer is assigned a number of congregations. Under that assignment of congregations, there is a responsibility for the organizer to go and build and develop a local organizing committee. And it's really forming teams of members that are willing and able to be active participants on these issues. We provide them workshops, training, and we organize them. Every LOC has super-leaders, people who really come to the surface and take leadership and then those become our captains at the congregations, and then it reaches a level where they become organizers themselves. The strategy is to build a structure with our organizers and the top leaders in our congregations so we can effectively disseminate information, train them, and mobilize them to be part of different efforts. Like when there's a particular policy proposed, we need to do phone banking, when we need to march, whatever we need to do, we have all those people that are not only ready to mobilize but they're also informed. We have a huge database, of all those people in every congregation, names and contact information and we use these databases when we do phone banking, when we do canvassing, and those things. And we have different levels of engagement—some leaders become super-leaders and they become part of a leadership table which is the most active—all of the ones in the immigration table are immigrants, and they really help us make decisions in terms of our organization and our agenda, and what are the things that we should prioritize.

This strategy is a bottom-up grassroots method centered on both congregations and lay leaders. Pastors are not required to publicly take on a campaign that might be controversial. The lay leaders of the congregational LOCs, not LA Voice, are the ones who decide what campaigns they choose to engage in. Once the decisions are made, LA Voice organizers simply train the lay leaders and facilitate the mobilization campaign.

In light of the immigration sweeps and mass detentions happening in Los Angeles County immediately after the Trump administration implemented its new enforcement policies, the congregational leaders in LA Voice's immigration table decided that mobilizing for SB54 was an important campaign to join. LA Voice mobilized the LOCs in their congregations to call voters, participate in public actions in support of SB54, picket in front of the sheriff's department to demand noncooperation with ICE, and visit city and county officials urging them to support the noncooperation of local law enforcement with ICE. According to Andrade,

> One issue that was of great concern to our table was the issue of the sheriff's department transferring immigrants to ICE. We mobilized a lot of picketing in front of the sheriff's office. And we invited a lot of media to make sure people heard what was happening. At the same time, we did a lot of phone-calling to different people—the sheriff's office, other public officials, the media, and just people in general of what was happening. And at many of those events, press conferences and picket lines we invited our clergy. And it's very powerful to have someone, you know, stand and speak on behalf of the faith community.

Brendan Busse, the Catholic priest leading the LA Voice LOC at Dolores Mission in East Los Angeles, became involved in the campaign for SB54. Through LA Voice, Fr. Busse was called into a meeting with then-governor Jerry Brown to urge him to sign the bill into law, partially because Fr. Busse is a Jesuit priest and Brown grew up in Jesuit circles. Fr. Busse describes the meeting:

> I was called into a meeting with Jerry Brown, governor at the time, to convince him to support the bill [SB54]. But also, we brought two young women we knew who had witnessed their own father being detained as he was trying to pick them up from school. And we had this immediate emotive, and personal impact in the room with the governor of California. I think the combination of those two things is powerful . . . sort of a clear mind about what the policy needs to do and also a clear heart about what's the right thing to do. Both of those in the same place. I think the most effective strategy is when you find ways to bring both of those things together. You need the narrative of the effect that it has and the clarity about what the systemic situation is that causes those effects. So, I think faith-based communities are uniquely positioned to do that because they have these networks and schools and universities and places where there's thinking and designing and alumni that are now in the legal profession and all of that. But you also have your feet in the ground where people are being directly affected by the systems that need to be changed.

This example shows a common pattern that we found in our interviews with faith-based advocacy organizations. They had personal relationships with people directly affected by Trump's immigration policy through their accompaniment work. Many faith-based advocacy organizations actually did accompaniment work during this time because so many people's lives were being disrupted by ICE enforcement policies. LA Voice at this time used their network of congregations to find homes for families in danger of being detained as well as recent asylum seekers being released as a result of their advocacy. These relationships then led into advocacy through powerful stories of the suffering caused by changes in policy.

Conclusion: The Advantages and Constraints of Faith-Based Advocacy

The three primary types of advocacy (direct lobbying, class-action lawsuits, and grassroots state and local organizing) that we discovered in our cases all show that one of the key advantages that faith groups have in advocacy is access to a significant number of volunteers in congregations willing to accompany and care for individuals who are suffering under the laws they are working to change. Our cases show that this can be a powerful component of advocacy if it is leveraged in the form of having those personal stories told to the media and to policy makers.

In the case of Pastor Luis Reyes, his connection to his denomination and other faith leaders who cared about him and his family led to a mobilization of faith leaders around the country to advocate for his release, which in turn exposed the extreme nature of Trump's enforcement priorities nationally in the media and mobilized a constituency that was willing to participate in subsequent advocacy campaigns. In the case of CLUE, congregation members willing to drive more than an hour each way to visit detainees at Adelanto on a regular basis to care for them and pray for them and also to document the abuses they were facing in detention led to powerful evidence used in class-action lawsuits that eventually prevailed. In the case of LA Voice, the personal connection Fr. Busse had with vulnerable immigrants targeted by ICE in the neighborhood of one of their member congregations provided a powerful in-person testimony at the governor's office when advocating for the Sanctuary State law.

This intersection of accompaniment and advocacy is not unique to faith-based organizations. Secular nonprofits also have deep personal relationships of care and accompaniment for their constituents that provide powerful stories used in advocacy. What is different is the access to large networks of volunteers in congregations that can provide much greater numbers of people willing to spend time with people, listen to them, pray for them, and care for their basic needs. This allows for more "boots on the ground" in terms of meeting with and caring for vulnerable or detained people, which expands the networks of people who know people with powerful personal stories, can tell those stories to fellow congregants, and can provide more passion and motivation to show up at protests, call public officials, and participate in letter-writing campaigns.

Faith-based advocacy also has the advantage of access to decision makers who share the faith of the advocates. The mobilization of networks of influential denominational leaders to lobby Chad Wolf to release COVID-19-vulnerable detainees shows the power of influential grasstops religious leaders acting in unison. In addition, the strategy of Matthew 25 / Mateo 25 leaders of forming long-term relationships with government officials in order to encourage them to follow the dictates of their faith and to transform them from opponents into allies is unique to faith-based organizing. In the case of Pastor Luis Reyes and other individual cases, those relationships with high-level officials, many of whom have personal faith commitments, and the use of scripture, prayer, and biblical concepts to call them to be faithful to a higher law of justice given by God seem to have influenced those with the power to release individuals. In the case of LA Voice, the meeting of Father Busse, a Jesuit priest, with Governor Jerry Brown, who grew up as a Jesuit Catholic, influenced the form that SB54 took and its passage. In the case of the Fullerton city council, public and private appeals based on faith led a city council member to decide not to support the Jeff Sessions lawsuit.

In sum, it is not just that these three advocacy strategies used by faith-based organizers are effective on their own; it is the ability of these networks of faith-based organizers to coordinate and combine all three strategies at once that makes them powerful. The groups that we have highlighted in this chapter all know each other and communicate regularly, and while their strategies may differ, they all recognize that the strategies of the others are useful and necessary and complement each other. One group can provide pastoral "discipling" of government officials, while others work with secular legal organizations to file class-action lawsuits and still others provide congregation members to make phone calls, write letters, and demonstrate in public. Working in concert, the community of faith-based organizers can have a tremendous impact by hitting policy makers and decision makers from all directions with multiple methods. According to one Matthew 25 / Mateo 25 leader, "You go multiple directions at once . . . it has to be surround sound." One official shared, "I feel like God is chasing me!"

The level of communication and cooperation among faith-based organizers and secular groups together, according to one Matthew 25 / Mateo 25 leader we interviewed, is somewhat unique to Southern California and emerged from the aftermath of the 1992 civil unrest following the verdict in the Rodney King case. According to this leader,

> The gift of Southern California is that this started after the civil unrest. It didn't exist before the unrest. Organizers came from all over the country to look at the Los Angeles miracle. What it really was is a miracle of conversation, communication. So, there was a meeting of leaders of LAANE [Los Angeles Alliance for a New Economy], HERE, CLUE, CHIRLA, and a lot of others including [civil rights leader] Jim Lawson. They all had breakfast together every two weeks. And out of that came the living wage movement, the first in the nation. That tradition of talking to each other has never been lost.

While other regions clearly have networks of cooperation between faith-based organizations protecting immigrants, and cooperation between faith-based and secular groups, the level of communication and cooperation in the Southern California network is unique because of the post-1992 history of relationship building (Flory, Loskota, and Miller 2011).

Yet while faith-based organizers working together with multiple methods have powerful potential for change, sometimes faith also presents obstacles to working together, limiting the impact of the work of faith-based advocates. Differences in the theology, political orientation, and cultures of different faith groups, including those led by immigrants, can lead to conflict and create obstacles for cooperation on campaigns. Evangelicalism, which is the fastest growing tradition among immigrant groups and second in popularity only to Catholicism among Latina/o immigrants, has a more individualistic theology that tends strongly toward either political conservatism or political disengagement. This theological orientation is rooted in Euro-American fundamentalism and has been transferred through the education that immigrant pastors receive from Euro-American-dominated denominations and institutions (Romero 2020). This sometimes cripples the organizing of immigrant evangelical congregations for political action, at least for causes deemed liberal. When Pastor Luis's case became public, some members of his largely politically conservative and white-led denomination, the Assemblies of God (AOG), were supportive of him personally and of his individual case but were hesitant to get involved in the larger campaign for immigrant advocacy or to challenge the policies of the Trump administration. Many immigrant pastors in this denomination were supporters of President Trump because of his positions on abortion and religious liberty and hesitant to criticize his immigration policies.

Some evangelical immigrant pastors have adopted an outright anti-immigrant stance similar to that of many white evangelical leaders. In 2018, we attended an event hosted by U.S. House representative Linda Sanchez (D-CA) to connect with religious leaders in her district for the purpose of educating and mobilizing support for changes in immigration policy. Some of the leaders she invited were pastors and faith-based nonprofit leaders who had reached out to her previously to strategize on how to protect DACA recipients. She also invited a group of Latino pastors from prominent congregations in her district. To her surprise, several of these prominent Latino evangelical pastors in her district confronted her and demanded that she do more to stop the flow of "illegals" into Southern California. Their suggestions included having the U.S. military stop them at borders within Central America.

These pastors, who led churches from conservative denominations, including Calvary Chapel and AOG, show the diversity of views on immigration and politics among immigrant religious leaders. Many

Latina/o evangelical pastors, particularly those connected to historically white U.S. evangelical denominations, such as AOG and Calvary Chapel, are strongly aligned with the Republican Party. In fact, an undocumented AOG pastor with whom we spoke who was detained by ICE told us that if he were allowed to vote, he would vote for Donald Trump because of his position on abortion. Nationwide in the 2020 election, Latina/o Protestants as a whole voted narrowly for Biden versus Trump (51–48 percent), compared to Latina/o Catholics, who voted overwhelmingly for Biden (71–28 percent). The Latino Religions and Politics National Survey, conducted in October 2020, found that Trump had more support than Biden did among Latina/o evangelicals (48 vs. 46 percent).

The political divide and hesitancy to advocate for immigrants is not limited to evangelical congregations, however. It exists across denominations, religious traditions, and racial/ethnic communities. The religious and political "culture war" of the United States exists within most congregations, even those with large immigrant constituencies.

Leaders from more traditional and politically conservative denominations also are sometimes hesitant to cooperate with more progressive religious groups on advocacy campaigns. While they may agree on advocating for vulnerable immigrants, they may have wide differences on other issues, such as LGBTQ rights, abortion rights, Black Lives Matter, and the police reform movement. This sometimes makes more traditional and conservative immigrant pastors uncomfortable working with progressive and largely white mainline Protestant groups that also advocate for some other issues they disagree with.

Last, religious differences are often an obstacle for cooperation between groups. As we have seen, one of the most powerful aspects of faith-based advocacy is using moral and religious language to advocate for those on the margins. This is a unique contribution that most secular groups cannot bring to advocacy campaigns. However, theological differences between religious groups often translate into different ways of using Scripture, worship styles, and moral language when advocating. CLUE, LA Voice, and other multifaith groups have worked hard to find moral language and scriptural references regarding justice that can unite multiple faith traditions in campaigns. A common phrase used in CLUE campaigns is "all religions believe in justice." More conservative, exclusivist traditions, however, are sometimes uncomfortable with this inclusive language. Many evangelicals, for example, are wary of the idea that their beliefs correspond to those of liberal mainline Protestants, let alone Muslims and Jews. For this reason, Matthew 25 / Mateo 25, which is led by Latina/o evangelicals, was formed to mobilize immigrant and nonimmigrant evangelicals and incorporates more specifically evangelical-style worship, biblical interpretations, and moral language. Matthew 25 / Mateo 25, while actively partnering with multifaith organizations on specific campaigns, offers a niche for evangelical pastors uncomfortable with more progressive theological and political language to mobilize for immigration reform.

These conflicts show that predominantly immigrant congregations, as well as predominantly white congregations, are situated in the religious and political divides and conflicts of the dominant European American culture in the United States. The phenomenon of immigrant-led congregations declining to participate in advocacy for immigrants because (1) they are politically conservative and do not want to oppose a conservative administration, (2) they differ politically or theologically from progressive congregations participating in immigrant advocacy, or (3) they are afraid of exposing their congregations to surveillance or policing by immigration authorities shows how constrained immigrant congregations are in a white-dominated society. These leaders and congregations, whether progressive or conservative, are part of white-dominated denominations and religious traditions and often adopt their worship styles, theological language, and political orientations and thus have inherited their political and religious conflicts. This leaves immigrant-led religious groups with barriers to unifying with each other to advocate for those vulnerable to being harmed by immigration policy and enforcement.

In the successful cases we have highlighted, overcoming the political and theological conflicts between religious groups was addressed in different ways. One approach is a network form of mobilization in which faith-based organizations can combine and recombine for individual campaigns but without formal alliances. For example, in the case of Pastor Luis, Matthew 25 / Mateo 25, which organizes mostly evangelical congregations, both immigrant and nonimmigrant, and AOG, a theologically and politically conservative white-led denomination, joined with more progressive multifaith nonprofits like CLUE and LA Voice for this particular campaign to free an evangelical immigrant pastor from unjust detention. These groups have continued to cooperate on other projects, such as the hunger strike to free COVID-19-vulnerable detainees at Adelanto, but they mobilize different constituencies and use varying theological language in that mobilization. When they come together for a public event, care is taken to (1) have mostly immigrant leaders speak and (2) avoid language that would alienate any of their constituencies. CLUE's Guillermo Torres, an immigrant himself, has roots in both mainline progressive and conservative evangelical traditions and therefore is able to thread this needle. This "separate but cooperative" strategy allows these nonprofits to stick to their primary constituencies' way of expressing their faith and politics but cooperate for specific campaigns where there is an overarching interest for all constituencies.

Another important aspect of overcoming the obstacles to cooperation is centering immigrant leadership and congregations. While significant numbers of white-led congregations participated in the successful campaigns that we have discussed, they were mostly in supporting roles. In the campaign to release Pastor Luis, white-led congregations participated in letter writing and meeting with ICE officials, but high-profile media campaigns and public events to mobilize action were led by mostly immigrant pastors who were sensitive to the political, cultural, and theological land mines that could potentially limit the participation of other immigrant pastors. In the case of CLUE, predominantly white congregations were involved in the Adelanto witness program but led by Guillermo Torres, who is well aware of the religious and political conflicts within immigrant congregations.

In the case of LA Voice, each congregation's LOC decides what campaigns are most important to their congregation and the LA Voice organizer follows the lead of the local LOCs. As a result, they are not trying to convince religious leaders to get involved in campaigns they are not comfortable with. Since a large percentage of the sixty congregations in the LA Voice network are in immigrant communities, the SB54 campaign resonated with many in their network, and therefore they actively wanted to join the campaign, despite its controversial nature. Thus, allowing congregational leaders in their network themselves to determine what campaigns to join avoids the problem of convincing leaders to join campaigns that would create problems for them.

In sum, we found the following dynamics in play in our analysis of faith groups doing advocacy. First, religious groups that can leverage their ability to mobilize congregational volunteers to personally accompany and care for individuals into advocacy campaigns have significant advantages compared to secular organizations. Second, religious groups that can gain access to key decision makers as a result of their common faith have an advantage over secular organizations in direct lobbying efforts directed at policy makers of faith. Third, a network model of mobilizing different religious traditions enables more effective advocacy by allowing for "wrap-around" campaigns using multiple methods and strategies simultaneously. This model requires significant investment in communication and relationship building across religious, political, and cultural divides. Fourth, centering immigrant leaders and organizations can overcome some of the political and theological divisions driven by the white-dominated religious and political culture wars in the United States. These four factors, we argue, account for much of the relative success of the faith-based advocacy campaigns that we highlighted above.

5

Education

Rev. Toña Rios has been a pastor for twelve years at Baldwin Park United Methodist Church—one of the UMC's flagship welcoming congregations—located in a majority Latina/o city eighteen miles east of downtown Los Angeles. Her journey as a pastor and faith-based organizer, however, began as a young adult in El Salvador under the guidance of Archbishop Oscar Romero. Toña recalls those formative years: "To speak of Monsignor Romero is to talk about a lot of things, but yes, I worked in that pastoral ministry at an early age because the situation that was taking place in the country was a situation where human rights were not respected. And my job was more than anything with the children and the youth. My job was especially in the Ahuachapán area, where the base communities began." Rev. Rios began organizing base communities among young people—groups of up to twenty who would meet informally, read the Bible together, and come up with ideas on how to apply the teachings of Jesus to their current situation. In particular, she began organizing young people to free youth who had been unjustly imprisoned by the Salvadoran government. "I worked especially with the young people who were in prisons for no reason . . . they always told us that there were young people who had arrested them. And we were looking for ways to find money where you could, making tamales, pupusas, doing whatever, so we could get those young people out. And it cost us a lot, it cost us a lot, but we did it. And we did it with pleasure, with enthusiasm to help the community."

As the civil war in the mid-1970s became more intense, Archbishop Romero and the Catholic Church began calling on the government to stop torturing, imprisoning, and killing its citizens suspected of being a part of the resistance movement. During this time Toña worked with the church to find refuge for families targeted by the government. As a result of this work, she was pursued by the government's death squads:

At a stronger time of war, something we also did strongly is find shelter for families. Get families out of the flames sometimes, from the hard times, try to move them and seek refuge. One of the blessings we had was the San Jose Mountain Seminary that Monsignor Romero opened. We said, "There is no shelter, there are no places for the families." And he said, "There's the seminary, right?" Then it was a pretty difficult, complicated job, but that made us strong too. And then sadly I appeared on a list of the death squads.

Because her life was now in danger, Toña decided to flee to Guatemala and was sheltered by members of a Catholic church there. While in Guatemala she received more death threats from the Salvadoran death squads, so she decided to flee to Mexico and from there crossed over into the United States. During this time, Archbishop Romero was assassinated.

During the 1980s, Toña became involved in the Sanctuary Movement, and through that movement she eventually learned how to apply for and gain legal residency. Her traumatic life experiences as well as the ways in which churches aided her and gave her the tools to advocate for herself and for others have profoundly shaped the work that she does today. Rev. Rios reflects on that time in her life:

The Sanctuary Movement in the eighties was something that opened the doors and helped a lot of people and I was one of them. In the process I realized that through that same Sanctuary Movement, they helped me to be able to apply to legalize myself, to legalize my status in this country. I think what we're now doing, and what many organizations and churches are also doing is copying part of that movement that was there before. That's what we're trying to do right now, to engage the community.

During her years as a community organizer in the Salvadoran community in the Pico Union district just west of downtown Los Angeles, she became acquainted with United Methodists doing advocacy work for immigrants. Because of her experiences with these Methodist activists, she eventually went to seminary and became a Methodist pastor. Currently, her ministry is one of the flagships of the UMC's Welcoming Congregations initiative.

One of the primary purposes that Toña sees for her ministry is continuing what she learned in El Salvador—educating people in practical ways to advocate for themselves using the base community method of organizing. In 2010 Toña mobilized base communities to protest against the Baldwin Park Police Department's practice of impounding the cars of undocumented immigrants for driving without a license and charging them exorbitant fees to retrieve their vehicles. If the driver could not pay the fees, they would auction off the car and keep the profits. This was before undocumented immigrants were allowed to get driver's licenses in California. The protests organized by Rev. Rios and others resulted in the city council prohibiting the police from impounding cars for the violation of driving without a license if a person with a license could pick it up and prohibiting charging fees for retrieving impounded cars (Himes 2010). After a California law was passed in 2013 (AB 60) that allowed undocumented immigrants to get driver's licenses, Toña's base communities then mobilized a highly successful campaign to educate her community on how to apply for one. Rev. Rios explains these educational campaigns:

> They took the cars from the residents and people couldn't afford those big fines they put on them, and the car got lost, right? They had car auctions and of course they were more expensive than we could afford. So, for things like these, if we look at what the gospel actually says, you must denounce injustices, right? And this is one of the injustices we had. Then people in our communities began to organize and fight for their rights. Then also, for example when we worked with the AB60 law, which is the driver's licenses, we began to organize people and we realized that many of our people who needed that license to take their children to school, or to take the child to work, many of those people could neither read nor write. So, to pass the test was super difficult. Then we started—let's make small groups—a base community. The center is Christ, and the base is all around you seeking that possibility of struggle. My church had several groups volunteering to help people take the exams and teaching them to read. We have people who still tell us, oh, thank you very much, we were able to get a license or glad that they have their job, because they have been able to do this.

Currently her congregation also operates a legal clinic that educates people on their rights as undocumented immigrants and helps them apply for DACA and legal residency. During the COVID-19 pandemic Toña also mobilized base communities in her church to pressure the city government to keep rents affordable and prevent evictions:

> We have the immigration clinics with help from different organizations. There are many people who do not know their rights. So, I went down to bring clinics here to the community. We have struggled for DACA for example, and the young people insist, in that terrible shadow in which they find themselves, to insist that there is sun for all, that the sun is born for all, but when the young people and their families do not have basic training, to put that idea into a young person, it has not been easy, right? However, we have managed to get these guys to apply for and renew their DACA permits.
>
> Right now, what's new is the city of Baldwin Park knows, knows and many of us know, this situation that we are living with this virus. They don't have a plan. But people are going to be hungry, they're going to lose their jobs or they're going to lose their homes, they're going to lose where they live. So, what's going to be the plan we're going to have as a city? And we asked, we talked to them, they don't have a plan. But when the first month passed, people began to say they already had been evicted from their houses. These families don't have a way to pay the rent. They had nothing, and people started telling the truth. We've lost the house, we've lost our jobs, we've lost our food. We've lost everything. Then we realized that the community must be organized, so we're right now organizing the community.

Toña's philosophy of educating her community for practical action in the face of their challenges is drawn from her long history of base community organizing and liberation theology. She explains this philosophy of education:

> I don't like the word "educate" but I like the word "truth." We need to understand the truth of the situations people live in. . . . People sometimes don't understand the terms we use very well. So, you have to get to the

population, you have to know where you live, you have to know who you live with because if you're talking up here and people are down here, they won't understand you and you're going to be left alone forever. And that's what happens to politicians. They leave our cities, they learn Spanish but they don't live it, and when we ask them questions directly, they say, "What? Tell me in another language because I don't understand you. What are you talking about?" So those people are not formed, we have no leaders, we have no leaders and the leader is made, not born. It has to be formed. So that's one of the very difficult things, there's no leadership and there are no people who are willing to form leaders among the people.

Toña then goes on to explain the base community method of educating and forming leaders.

We see that what works in communities are small groups. Start with small groups to talk to people. It's my turn to talk one at a time . . . and each person's answers are different, but here comes that training, right, to train people in a way that they can understand that their need is my need, that their pain is my pain, right? Because a lot of people talk about books. He talks about what he's read, but he doesn't talk about his personal experience. Everything starts with two. With two people and a prayer or a biblical text an agenda is developed based on the need that has been raised, or something that someone said. So, it's the same model and it all starts there. It doesn't matter who we're going to meet, but we start with a prayer. Sometimes it occurs in these moments, right, because in the agenda we have the prayer at the beginning. So, we're a faith group, we're not a political group. We are not a group that was born out there, but we are a group of faith who lives here. From there we bring the initiative and we will work together. So that's the idea of starting from that little group. Two people start the initiative, and then we now come together to organize, right? So, we will organize ten thousand people, but we will start with two or three that are going to start working together. And now we have the blessing that there are many young people who are excited. Perhaps they do not have very concrete ideas yet, but if someone helps them organize, they become very good ideas.

This grassroots educational strategy of small prayer and Bible study groups educating each other in the needs of the community by sharing their own stories, needs, and pain and the stories of those they live with has proven effective not only in Rev. Rios's congregation but throughout Latin America. Her base community strategy is one model of faith-based education for social change that we witnessed in our case studies.

Religion, Education, and Organizing Social Movements

Educating and training leaders in the practical tools of organizing is a key component of any social movement. The term "community organizing" usually refers to the techniques for pursuing social change developed by Saul Alinsky in the 1930s (Wood 2002; Salvatierra and Heltzel 2014). Alinsky's model for organizing emphasized person-to-person meetings, using conflict and tension strategically, and the importance of movements being led by people who are most affected by a particular policy (Wood 2002). Key to this strategy is appealing to the self-interest of those most affected by oppressive policies. Often, faith-based organizing applies many of the same principles of the Alinsky model but gives a religious rationale for doing so (Wood 2002). Salvatierra and Heltzel (2014) make the distinction between faith-based organizing, which mostly follows the Alinsky model, and "faith-rooted" organizing, which draws less on self-interest and more heavily on "the deepest wells of the beliefs, values, disciplines, and practices" of faith communities for tactics and motivation. Yukich (2013) demonstrated that the target of the New Sanctuary Movement of the mid-2000s was as much an attempt to change religious institutions to reflect their deepest values as it was an effort to change state policy, thus showing that faith-rooted organizing can and often is something different from simply applying religious resources and motivations to the Alinsky model.

In our cases, we saw a wide array of techniques to educate and train people for the work of protecting immigrants, many of which drew from or are compatible with the Alinsky model but also drew from motivations and tactics that were based on the highest ideals of their faith. In our cases, we observed that most of them fell into three models of education and training that we have labeled (1) base community, (2) religious leader education, and (3) direct service.

Base Communities: Baldwin Park UMC and Dolores Mission

The base community model of education and training grew out of the liberation theology movement in Latin America in the 1970s. Base communities were developed mostly in rural areas and were led by lay Catholic leaders. Base communities met in groups of around ten to twenty, studied the scriptures, especially the teachings of Jesus, and then prayed and thought about how to apply the teachings of Jesus in their communities. Base communities taught peasants basic skills like reading and writing along with religious teachings in an effort to empower and liberate them (Hillar 1993). From these groups, marginalized people were able to organize and create a sense of unity and power to advocate for themselves to change their lives for the better (Tombs 2002).

The base community model of educating for the work of protecting immigrants in our cases is illustrated in the example of Rev. Toña Rios's Baldwin Park United Methodist Church. As we saw earlier, the UMC's Welcoming Congregations initiative is a place-based strategy, leveraging Methodist properties in immigrant communities to establish ministries that serve their immediate neighbors in whatever way seems appropriate. This fits well with the base community strategy of training community members in the neighborhood in which the church resides. Rev. Rios simply gathers small groups of community members to pray, read scripture, and talk about their experiences and the most pressing concerns of their lives. As it turned out in the 2010s, the most pressing concerns of many of the people in these small groups were having their cars impounded by the police and passing the driver's license test. In 2020, it was getting evicted because of the pandemic. She took these concerns on as if they were her own and helped these small groups learn how to take their concerns to decision makers in their city. These concerns would probably not be on the radar of an organizer who did not live in her community or one who was not deeply entwined in the daily lives of her constituents.

Another one of our cases that used the base community model is the Catholic Dolores Mission Parish in East Los Angeles. Father Brendan Busse helped organize base communities in the neighborhood parish and through this method was introduced to people whose lives were dramatically altered by the Trump administration's immigration enforcement changes. The mission has been using the base communities model to organize their community since the 1980s. According to Fr. Busse,

> In the eighties there were a lot of Salvadorian refugees being taken in by a largely Mexican population here in the neighborhood. And that was at the beginning a very informal project inspired and moved by the base community model. The Jesuits when they got here to the parish adopted the base community model. And those base communities—each one sort of chipped in to figure out different issues they think they could work on in the parish. It was rooted in getting small communities of parishioners together when possible. And after reading the gospel asking themselves, how that gospel interacts with and implicates their own living situation, their own social reality. It's essentially a model of parish leadership where instead of a hierarchical model where the pastor has an advisory council that then gets shared out to different ministries, you form small communities, usually based in corners of the neighborhood where people who can live near each other can just gather together every week and just go through that simple scriptural analysis of read the gospel for the coming Sunday and ask the question "What would Jesus see in our situation? What would Jesus feel about it? What would Jesus do about it?" And then "what are we asked to do if we're to be the body of Christ in this place?" And that simple question leads to instead of one person's idea trying to get filtered out into a million different ways, it's a bunch of people with different ideas kind of developing organically in a plurality of ministries. It leads to different versions of ministry within the neighborhood that then becomes sustained by the question—not what should the pastor do but what can we do in order to live the way that Jesus wants us to live. Presuming you have a cooperative and encouraging pastor, the pastor follows the lead of the people, not the other way around.

This base community model led Dolores Mission to use part of their property to house people in their local community who were in danger of deportation in the 1980s, and now this housing is used both for unhoused members of their community and for asylum seekers. The base community model of organizing also led Fr. Busse to develop deep connections to people in his neighborhood, some of whom were feeling the effects of the Trump administration's new immigration enforcement regime. This led Dolores Mission to develop a grassroots rapid response network through their base communities, which educated people in their neighborhood on what to do if they were encountered by ICE officers. Fr. Busse explains,

> We created community-based rapid response networks that empower the community to feel like, even if we can't change the law at this point or even if we can't keep up with the abuses around the law that are happening, we can build resiliency within the community. I think that's a victory—because sometimes the legal work is doing the work for the community. It's hard for community members who aren't lawyers to do some of that work. But a rapid response network where you have support groups and doing trainings about how to report abuses of law enforcement and knowing your rights. Those are all big, big victories because they have the effect immediately. It's not something you have to wait for long-term systemic change to happen to have a community that feels resilient and addresses some of the trauma and anxiety of being persecuted all the time.

Fr. Busse's statement sums up the base community model of educating/ training community members. It does not require formal education, like law degrees, to do the work. It does not mean waiting for changes in the law to empower community members. And it does not wait for the priest to decide what needs to be done and organize training sessions to mobilize people. All it takes is getting people together and sharing personal challenges and a motivation to follow Jesus's command to love their neighbors. It is community members who do the work and then educate the priests in the parish as to what is happening. The priests can then draw on their resources to support the work that the base communities are doing to help their neighbors.

Delores Mission also provides legal counsel to undocumented community members through a relationship with Loyola Marymount Law School in Los Angeles. The congregation is also part of LA Voice's network and, as noted earlier, participated in that group's campaign for the Sanctuary State law, SB54. As a result of the base community model, Fr. Busse and the other leaders at Dolores Mission have deep ties to the community surrounding Dolores Mission. These ties, along with the connection to LA Voice, were used to connect individuals whose families were separated by Trump's enforcement policies to Governor Jerry Brown and his staff. This had an influence on the governor's support for the bill.

Educating Religious Leaders: Matthew 25 / Mateo 25

The second model of education and training we witnessed in our cases was the strategy of educating pastors and religious leaders to mobilize their congregations. Immigrant religious leaders, in particular, are an important strategic group in the movement to defend and protect immigrants for a number of reasons. First, their communities are the ones most affected by immigration enforcement policies. Their congregations often contain vulnerable undocumented immigrants with whom they have an intimate connection and knowledge of their struggles. Second, as immigrants themselves, they have a level of legitimacy and inside knowledge that nonimmigrant leaders do not have. Third, they have social capital—deep networks of pastors outside of their congregation that they can mobilize for action.

Many immigrant pastors, however, are reluctant to engage in public actions to advocate for immigrants or challenge the immigration system for several reasons. First of all, many of them are bivocational—they do not earn enough money as pastors for that to be their full-time job. Thus, it is difficult enough for these pastors to have time to do the work of preaching, organizing worship services, and praying for and meeting the spiritual needs of their members, let alone take on the difficult tasks of accompaniment and advocacy. Second, undocumented immigrants often make up a significant percentage of their congregations—therefore they sometimes choose not to bring up the issue because of the fear it would open up a flood of needs that they would not know how to meet and therefore become overwhelmed. Third, many are reluctant because immigration is a controversial issue even in predominantly immigrant congregations. The theological perspective of many Christian traditions places a high value on obedience to the law—therefore undocumented members of their congregations may feel shame or embarrassment because of their status in a church setting and therefore do not want people to know their status and struggles. Conversely, congregational members who have legal residency status may look down upon or judge members who do not have legal status. In addition, many church members and some pastors, especially in evangelical and Catholic congregations, may identify more with conservative political perspectives and therefore may be sympathetic to Republican anti-immigrant rhetoric, even if they are immigrants or are undocumented themselves. Last, many of these pastors do not want to stand out and identify themselves as immigration activists because they do not want their congregations to be targeted by ICE or by anti-immigrant groups. Thus, significant barriers exist to convincing immigrant pastors to engage in immigration advocacy.

There is also a need to educate nonimmigrant religious leaders. Most U.S. residents are unaware of the way the immigration system works or of the difficulties and traumas that are inflicted by the system. The popular refrain of "why don't they just come legally?" or "they should get in line like the rest of us did" belies their ignorance of the poverty and violence that many immigrants are fleeing and the near impossibility for most people of migrating legally to the United States. Most people are also unaware of the harm that the system places on families that are separated or the abusive conditions in immigration detention centers. Thus, many of our cases prioritize educating nonimmigrant religious leaders and congregations in hopes that religious values of compassion, justice, and the common humanity of all people under God would create empathy for the suffering of those trying to migrate and therefore motivate action among nonimmigrant believers. This is also a hard task because of the emphasis of most religions on obedience to the law and the tendency of white Christians in the United States to affiliate with the Republican Party, which pushes anti-immigrant narratives to win votes. Thus, for both immigrant and nonimmigrant religious groups, educating and training for immigration advocacy is difficult and controversial and therefore something most religious leaders do not participate in.

Soon after Matthew 25 / Mateo 25 was formed in the wake of the 2016 election, Matthew 25 / Mateo 25 leaders began holding education training sessions for immigrant pastors and leaders. Immediately after the election, the focus was on training pastors and leaders of immigrant congregations to help their undocumented members know their rights. Subsequently, when detention of undocumented immigrants began to increase, legal help and in some cases public pressure campaigns were organized for some of the individuals who were detained, deported, and separated from their families. Matthew 25 / Mateo 25 then began forming support circles—partnerships between immigrant and nonimmigrant churches to house and accompany asylum seekers. All of this required education and training of pastors willing to lead their congregations into this difficult and controversial work.

In 2019 Matthew 25 / Mateo 25 established a partnership with the evangelical Fuller Theological Seminary in Pasadena to provide formal training for immigrant pastors wanting to advocate for the vulnerable immigrants in their congregations and communities. This led to a six-month certificate program for pastors and church leaders called the Diplomado Superior Respuesta de la Iglesia a la Crisis Migratoria, or simply Diplomado. This program trains pastors and lay leaders to do immigration advocacy and accompaniment work. The program consists of online training videos, including sessions on immigration law, trauma care, building partnerships with other organizations, preparing a congregation to do accompaniment, and providing a theological basis for welcoming and protecting immigrants. The program is unique in the evangelical seminary world and now has participants in fifteen different countries in Latin America.

While other denominations and groups, such as the Catholic Diocese of Los Angeles, train pastors to do immigration work, the Fuller Diplomado program has several unique aspects. First of all, while the program provides options for English-speaking pastors in the United States and Latin America, it is centered upon educating and training Spanish-speaking immigrant pastors in the United States. The coursework is all in Spanish, and all of the educators are first- or second-generation Latina/o Christian leaders who have been doing immigration advocacy for a decade or more. Second, rather than training the pastor or leader individually, the program requires that the leader do the training in conjunction with a group of other leaders in their church. Alexia Salvatierra, a key founder of the program, explains the importance of this communal aspect of the training program: "You have to have a collegial imagination, because the pastor doesn't run the church by him- or herself. They run it first with their extended family and, secondly, with a network of leaders that are like family. And if the pastor goes through this whole experience at school and he gets a new vision, but the church doesn't have the vision it's not going to happen."

In order to accommodate this collectivist approach to leading a congregation, the program requires that the pastor or leader do the training in conjunction with other people from their congregation or community. They meet together, watch the videos together, and discuss how to put the principles into practice together. The pastor and members of the congregation in the training program meet once a month with a coach and talk about what is happening in their congregation and brainstorm ideas of how to implement practices learned in the program with the coach. The coach is provided by the program and has experience doing faith-based immigration advocacy. Some are previous graduates of the Diplomado program who have established effective immigration advocacy programs in their congregations. The Diplomado program leaders reason that this collectivist approach is much more likely to result in congregations actually doing immigration work after the program is over than if a pastor were to go through the program alone.

Dr. Salvatierra explains why the program's educators are all Latina/o, most of whom have done immigration advocacy work in the context of churches: "You need to see that people like you can do something . . . you have to have a sense that someone you can relate to as part of your larger circle is able to do this, and most of them are people who also have done the work in their congregations so they're giving their own testimony." Another unique requirement of the Diplomado program is that at least one of the congregation members who joins the pastor or leader in the training program must be under thirty years old. Dr. Salvatierra explains this requirement: "The young leaders are encouraged to go out and experiment with different kinds of activities like going to a march, going along on a visit to a legislator, so they can bring that back and say you know look I did this—we can do it." Typically, young people in congregations are much more likely to want to engage in social and political action on behalf of immigrants, while the older leaders in the church are much more reluctant. In fact, in our research we found that young people in many immigrant congregations are often frustrated with the older leadership for not doing more to protect the immigrants in their congregation and more generally to get involved in pursuing social change. The Diplomado program attempts to address these generational conflicts by working through them together with a coach.

Dr. Salvatierra explains some of the reluctance, particularly with older and evangelical pastors and leaders, to get involved in any kind of political advocacy work:

> You still have all the issues around the idea that we don't get involved in the political sphere. You know, we are hesitant—we're suspicious of movements. The kids are, you know, a powder keg ready to become militant but the parents are not. It's like they had the immigrant experience, but they're keeping their heads down, most of them. It's controversial. There isn't a church that's been involved where it's not a controversy. It gets into social justice stuff which you know the white evangelicals that they're in relationship with have told them not to do. So, it feels rebellious and there's some people in the congregation, they don't like it that other people in the congregation are undocumented, and for some people who are undocumented it feels like it puts them at risk to deal with it directly. It's like it's let's just pretend it doesn't exist, because, maybe somebody will find out about us.
>
> And then there's the trauma and all the mental health care is highly controversial. Even though the people love it so much because they're like "my people are in so much pain." You know, we have kids that stopped being able to study at school because their mothers are deported and we just really need to know how to do this. But it's still a big stigma that you can't just pray it away. Like what's wrong with you? You should be able to call in the Holy Spirit and everybody should be fine. So those are all parts of an inherited faith from certain strands of evangelicalism and Pentecostal faith that are not helpful.

Despite the controversies involved in the work of caring for and protecting vulnerable immigrants in their congregations and communities, many pastors and leaders of predominantly immigrant congregations are motivated because of the deep suffering that exists in their congregations. The Diplomado program provides leaders the knowledge and tools to engage in the work and a space to address their fears.

Manuel "Manny" Arteaga, an alumnus of Fuller's Diplomado program, is the lead pastor of Kaleo Adventist Church in Glendale, a bilingual "Spanglish" Latina/o congregation made up of mostly immigrants from a wide variety of backgrounds and cultures. Manny migrated from Mexico when he was thirteen years old. He remembers his childhood church in the United States as a place of warm community but a place that did not help him process his immigrant experience as a teen:

> Even though my experience was not the usual trauma that we talk about—like the coyotes or crossing through the desert—we had a visa and we just overstayed—it was still traumatic in the sense that there was a sense of displacement, there was a sense of, you know where do I belong, who am I, you know, an identity crisis. And the church had nothing to say. In my own identity crisis, I started acting a fool. And all the church did was say, "Oh look—he shaved his head he's now becoming like one of them here, you know, and you know he just came from Mexico and now he's bad and his pants are baggy. You know he's getting Americanized" and that's all they could offer is criticism, never any support.

As he continued in church through adulthood, he decided to study to become a pastor in the Adventist tradition he grew up in and received his first call as a pastor to a Latina/o immigrant congregation near MacArthur Park, just west of downtown Los Angeles. Similar to his church growing up, he says, his ministry offered no help to people in processing their immigrant experience. "Ninety-nine percent of the congregation was immigrant and I think a good 80 percent undocumented and we had nothing, nothing to say about their immigrant experience, nothing to offer other than just one another—community—but nothing really intentional. . . . Not even in our preaching—a lot of it was so high and lofty but never really speaking to the immigrant experience." Manny explains why most immigrant congregations, at least in the Adventist tradition, offer no help in navigating the immigrant experience, other than providing a close community of people with similar experiences:

> My denomination it's beautiful, I mean Adventists are all about the expectation and the arrival of Jesus right, so we place a strong emphasis on Jesus that came and died for me and saves me and I'm going to be with him someday and it's this in that moment there's this beautiful longing that as a community, we have for that day. But that has a slippery slope, because

we can become escapist. We can become so fixated on that day that we forget that we neglect the implications of being a follower of Christ today. What does that mean when I find out that there's twenty-five hundred unaccompanied minors in Pomona Fairplex right now? What does that call me to do? And that's the connection that really wasn't there growing up. There's that disconnect of longing for heaven and longing to be with Jesus and what about today, what does that look like today. We haven't done well as a denomination to make that connection quite yet and I'm trying at my local church.

Over the years as a pastor and as an immigrant himself, he has longed to help people navigate the trauma, the displacement, the identity crisis that people face in their migration journeys, but felt like he didn't have the knowledge to know how to begin. When he saw the Fuller Diplomado program advertised on social media, he immediately signed up and was part of the first cohort of Latina/o pastors in 2019.

When asked how the program affected his ministry, he speaks of a theological paradigm shift:

I love the shift that my theology took, you know, in my preaching and in my teaching. I became more aware. I became more intentional about connecting the pulpit to the pew in my preaching in my public ministry. Looking at how [Fuller professor Oscar Garcia-Johnson] would take scripture—he does so beautifully—he would take scripture and he would read it through an immigrant lens that for some reason I was trying to put away. I just remember being there just floored by how he would read the text through that perspective and that helped model for me and I've been trying to work on that part of my craft ever since.

This paradigm shift that he attributes to his time at the Fuller Diplomado resulted in changes not only in his preaching and teaching but also in church programming. Knowing that his church members are holding significant trauma from their migration experiences, he has started an emphasis on trauma care and mental health:

The month of July we are having a mental health sermon series where the pastor is not preaching—I'm bringing mental health experts that are going to be tackling attachment and trauma. As long as I'm in this church we're going to make that a priority and part of my goal is to be able to have ten or fifteen thousand dollars a year to help subsidize therapy for people in my church and by next year have 15 percent or 20 percent in therapy and just keep growing that number every year. And to make that conversation central to what we do as a church was a seed that was planted in those Diplomado sessions about trauma and the psychological effects of migration with [Fuller professor Dr. Lisseth Rojas-Flores].

In addition to the new emphasis on mental health and trauma care, Manny has enlisted volunteers from his congregation to address the needs of recent immigrants in his community—including visiting unaccompanied minors and welcoming recent refugees and asylum seekers from Afghanistan.

The transitions that Manny has initiated since his completion of the Diplomado program, however, have not all gone smoothly. The COVID-19 pandemic and losing the lease on their building, which caused them to move to a more distant location, put the congregation in what Manny calls "survival mode." He also experienced pushback from some of his congregation as his preaching has changed to addressing racial injustice and immigration. Some families have left for this reason, and others have criticized him on their blog posts and YouTube channels:

The fact that I was very vocal about certain things made me lose a lot of people. I lost entire families, because I spoke up during the George Floyd uprising and all that, I marched and I was vocal about being antiracist and I lost entire families just gone. Right now, I think we are operating with about 40 percent of what we used to be. You know it hit us financially.

They associate all that with the left, and these are not left-leaning people. They may be Latinos, but they are very much influenced by right-wing ideologies and theologies—you know, really heavy on law enforcement and military and stuff like that and very, very heavily influenced by the right-wing political talking points. So, everything from vaccines to masks and racism and immigration.

I've heard the blog posts, and you know the comments about me in YouTube videos from people in my church. When I have spoken about immigration I've gotten a lot of criticism for it—I need to stick to the

Gospel and not talk about these political things. So yeah, sadly it comes with a package, right? We're there as a society where, if you talk about this then you are woke and you are this and that. But I'm just trying to stay faithful to Jesus man and, as I read my Bible, as I get into scripture as Jesus comes alive in me that's how I like to preach and that's what I preach from. If you don't like it then take it up with him. I keep it real like that, but yeah it doesn't line up with some of their views so I've gotten a lot of pushback.

For Manny, the years since he completed the Diplomado have been exhausting because of navigating COVID-19, transitioning to a new church location, and losing 60 percent of his congregation, partially due to the criticisms and pushback he has received since his participation in the Diplomado. He is committed to continuing on the path, however, inspired by the vision of Jesus and the Kingdom of God on earth that became clearer because of his participation in the program.

In addition to educating immigrant leaders in how to protect and care for vulnerable immigrants, Matthew 25 / Mateo 25 and Fuller's Diplomado have also prioritized educating nonimmigrant leaders from predominantly nonimmigrant congregations. Key to the vision of Matthew 25 / Mateo 25 is the engagement of nonimmigrant congregations to change hearts and minds for the long-term goal of immigration reform.

In 2018, when caravans of asylum seekers were arriving at the Tijuana–San Diego border, Matthew 25 / Mateo 25 organized trips to Tijuana for nonimmigrant Christian leaders to see for themselves what was happening at the border in contrast to the fear-evoking media portrayals that were ubiquitous at the time. Matthew 25 / Mateo 25 formed partnerships with evangelical churches in Tijuana that were sheltering some of the asylum seekers coming in the caravans and brought nonimmigrant leaders from the United States to Tijuana to connect with these asylum seekers, hear their stories, and see some of the conditions at the makeshift camps at the border. One of the purposes of these trips is to encourage U.S.-based nonimmigrant leaders to embrace a posture of learning while centering Latino faith leaders on both sides of the border. According to Vanessa Martinez, one of the main organizers of the Matthew 25 / Mateo 25 trips to the border, "We learn from the leadership of the Mexican leaders and even from the leadership or a lot of the asylum seekers who have had to stay longer than they should because of the unfair policies and rules. The trips are to teach us . . . to recenter them into the story." This posture of learning is not always embraced by white pastors and leaders during these trips, making this educational work difficult for the Latina/o leaders involved. Martinez elaborates on the dynamic of educating white Christian leaders, whether conservative evangelical or progressive mainline, who are used to being in charge and used to imparting knowledge rather than gaining it from others:

> Some of the [white U.S. pastors] would go and talk to the [Mexican] pastor and give her suggestions—but [they] have never run a shelter. It was just very traumatic for me, right. Because I'm trying to protect people who are already dealing with this trauma. And I have people who think they're actually doing us a favor by, you know, using their white privilege or their American mindset of what they think should be done, thinking that they're helping but they're not.
>
> It was very difficult to give instructions when we were at the border camps. Don't argue with authorities. If they tell you not to do something, don't do it. Your American rights are not going to be protected. That can create conflict with the Mexican pastors and leaders who were accompanying us and opening up the doors for us because if [the Mexican authorities] see us being like this, they're going to blame them and not us because they have to stay, we get to leave. And so, there were various times where [a white leader] would approach me and ask me a question only to let me know something they were going to do. Because even if I told them that is not wise, this isn't safe for you to do or this isn't safe for the people that you're doing it with. It doesn't honor their dignity. They would still do it. So, I would have to find out and have to go and intervene. One time a group of white Christians were "moved by the Holy Spirit" to give money to some asylum seekers but not others; which would lead to internal conflict that the Mexican pastors at the shelter would need to deal with after our groups left. I had to physically use my body to get in the middle and say things like "you can't give this person money because the Holy Spirit led you to do it."

Some attempts of progressive white leaders to show their "allyship" with Mexican leaders also did not land well, according to Martinez:

It was very stressful because it was really hard, at least for me personally, to deal with white liberals, in their attempt to be allies. They would speak out against the American government, you know, and all of its unfairness to the folks in the Tijuana—how do you tell somebody who's already been oppressed by this empire—they already know these things. So, it was unnecessary and it was more to make themselves feel better, you know, or to make themselves feel less guilty.

In part because of these difficulties, Matthew 25 / Mateo 25 no longer takes groups of nonimmigrant leaders to the border for educational trips. However, the education of nonimmigrant congregational leaders has been incorporated into the Diplomado program at Fuller seminary. The program has an English-speaking track for predominantly English-speaking Latina/o congregations and another English-speaking track for predominantly white and multiracial congregations. These cohorts watch the same training videos, but their assignments and exercises are different in order to address the distinctive issues based on their contexts and to address the issue of centering Latina/o leaders in doing the work of protecting immigrants.

Direct Service Model: Southern California Immigration Task Force of the Catholic Church

The third model of educating immigrant communities we have called the direct service model. This model entails faith-based nonprofit organizations directly providing educational services to immigrants or congregation members. Often a church will host these trainings, but an outside organization will provide the educational event on topics such as know-your-rights workshops, applying for DACA, and trainings on how to apply for asylum or how to petition to get a loved one out of detention. These are often onetime events that happen sporadically, therefore limiting the number of people who can participate. But they also tend to have the capacity to serve large numbers of people at one time because staff are trained in educating large groups and communities.

The Southern California Immigration Task Force of the Catholic Church was founded through the leadership of Isaac Cuevas, the director of immigration and public affairs for the LA Diocese's Office of Life,

Justice, and Peace. This task force draws Catholic priests and lay leaders from four different Southern California dioceses—Los Angeles, San Bernardino, Orange, and San Diego—who are interested in providing education to their congregations and communities regarding immigration. In many cases, this means providing educational services directly to immigrant communities.

The task force holds leadership workshops every fall and spring to educate priests and lay leaders on current issues in immigration policy and enforcement. They then take this knowledge to their communities. The task force also provides workshops to educate immigrant communities directly. According to Isaac Cuevas,

> And in that leadership workshop basically it's kind of like a presentation of what the office is doing and what our initiatives are for the year. . . . We then create programs and initiatives where we can go back to parishes and utilize their networks and their reach locally to get more people to come. We've done know-your-rights workshops. We've done citizenship workshops. We've done DACA renewal application workshops. We've done so when TPS was rescinded by the president. We did workshops to help people renew their TPS and reminded them to do so.
>
> One of our most recent programs has actually been a passport workshop . . . the State Department actually reached out to us. They saw something in the *LA Times* that we had done and they came to us with a problem which was children, U.S.-born children, were winding up at U.S. embassies in other parts of the world. Their parents, who were undocumented and either had been deported or had chosen to self-deport, did so in such a hurry, or sometimes by the situation, that they never bothered to get passports for their children and now they were showing up at U.S. embassies, knocking at the door saying: here's my son's birth certificate and here's my son. How do you prove that that document and that child match up? Well, if you at least go through the process here of getting a passport for that child, it establishes direct citizenship and is a document that they can use for the rest of their life, even if it expires. But it establishes the process and protocol here that this person is a valid U.S. citizen. Otherwise, what you wind up having a person who is undocumented in another country and they're a U.S. citizen.

We did one workshop in August of last year and I asked the State Department what would be a good number and they said if we could do a hundred passports in a day, that would be huge. We were able to process 278 passports in one day. And again, these are families. We opened it up wide to anyone and everyone who wanted and could attend. It was really successful.

We did this at a local parish. The beauty about this was that we were very strategic . . . this was a U.S. passport workshop—come get your U.S. passport, it's the most American thing you can do aside from voting. Right, like you need to have a passport, be responsible and nobody can really say anything against that, right? Covertly, we also worked with our immigrants' rights groups to kind of spread it word of mouth and go to our undocumented communities and say hey look, if you have a U.S.-born child and they don't have a passport yet, let us help you and you don't need to have your legal status . . . we're the church you can trust us and that's really where the magic happened. It was through our networks and through our leadership that we've been able to have such a tremendous amount of people show up and it being the Catholic church, they obviously trust that the process is going to be safe and adequate and they won't have to worry. When we did the workshop in San Diego, we had a reporter come out and they said, "My gosh! I just recently did a passport thing over at the federal building and this feels so much different than it feels at the federal building because everyone here at this church wants to help you through every single process whether it's the photo or the application or just the act of giving you snacks while you wait is such a kind thing to do at the parish. When you go to the federal building, if you fill something out wrong, they make you feel like you're just the dumbest person on earth and *why are you wasting people's time.* Just the feeling of one thing versus the other is so different. The value is just tremendous, especially for the people who aren't used to navigating our complex systems."

This passport workshop shows the advantages of faith-based organizations in educational programming. They used the networks of parish priests to inform undocumented families about the necessity of getting their U.S. citizen children passports and provided an event at a local parish. Having the workshop take place in a local Catholic church eliminated the fear that some families had about approaching a federal government building offering the same services. As undocumented immigrants, they trusted the church more than the government, and the church was able to mobilize volunteers to make the event a welcoming and hospitable environment.

Parish priests find it helpful that the task force provides educational events and guest speakers for their Sunday services as well. Many of the parish priests are for immigration reform and advocating for undocumented immigrants but are afraid to bring up the topic because of the fear of a backlash from conservative members of the congregation, even in predominantly immigrant congregations. Therefore, the fact that the Catholic hierarchy supports and provides these services and pro-immigrant guest speakers from the diocese gives legitimacy in the eyes of the congregation.

One of the parish priests we interviewed explained the reluctance of priests to bring up immigration at mass: "Even in our church to preach on immigration is a controversial thing. You can get attacked and so that's an obstacle. And there's a tendency for a lot of pastors to not even want to touch it. Pastors are not generally prophets. You can't really be an out-and-out prophet in our perish, because prophets are divisive, and so a lot of pastors run from the topic, because it creates conflict so that's a big obstacle."

One lay leader in the task force, attorney Linda Grimm, provides pro bono legal help to asylum seekers but also at times serves as a guest speaker in parishes on Sundays. She concurs:

The hierarchy of my faith community sees itself as motivating people [to support immigrants], but I wager that if you went to mass at every parish in the Archdiocese of LA for six months you wouldn't hear anybody preach about immigration. You wouldn't hear it mentioned, even if the scripture readings for the day you know cry out for it because you know perhaps a story of somebody's migration. The hierarchy in their public face, they take great comfort in the fact that catholic charities and religious sisters and all the laypeople are accompanying people one by one but they never speak out about the violation of law or inhumane things that the [Trump] administration is doing, for example, and I never hear them talking about the consistent ethic of life or how the unborn and the immigrant child on the other side of the border are both human beings with dignity, you just don't hear that kind of talk at mass.

The Southern California Immigration Task Force of the Catholic Church has used the Catholic hierarchical structure strategically in educating and training for immigrant advocacy in the face of resistance from people in the pews. They use the LA Diocese Office of Life, Justice, and Peace to network with priests and lay leaders who want to engage in this work, then use their office to provide educational services directly to immigrants, while using the community connections of parish priests to reach out to those who need the educational services provided by the task force. Therefore, the priest does not have to engage in the work of educating directly or mobilizing their divided congregations to do the work. While this strategy does not attempt to convince parishioners to support immigrants or immigration reform, it provides key practical information and training for the most vulnerable immigrants themselves.

CLUE, another one of our cases, also provides direct education to congregations at Sunday services to educate nonimmigrant members about the immigration system. They often bring asylum seekers to services to tell their stories in order to illustrate the injustices that exist in the system. Guillermo Torres, immigration program director for CLUE, describes how his organization provides direct educational services to churches, congregations, and synagogues on the plight of asylum seekers:

Faith communities are not aware of why asylum seekers are coming to seek asylum and refugees. To let them know about the horrible conditions of people whose lives are at risk, we go to many different congregations and we give a little narrative of the current situation in those countries. . . . Right now, we're speaking about Central America, what is known as the Northern Triangle region, which is Guatemala, El Salvador, and Honduras. . . . So, we go to congregations and let them know why people are leaving those countries and why they are seeking asylum. We also try to give a biblical perspective from the Old Testament or the New Testament. God's view on immigrants versus human views, or the current political views on both sides of the aisle. And the reason why Christ died, is that everybody is desirable. Everyone has dignity, right? And that these policies have no sense of humanity, no sense of compassion, no sense of dignity, and no connection at all to those suffering among us that goes against all the values that God is for which are mercy, compassion, and justice, and truth.

By appealing to biblical notions of compassion, mercy, and justice, Christian advocacy organizations try to humanize immigrants and thereby dispel ignorance and prejudice surrounding immigration. Guillermo Torres describes how they connect people of faith to the asylum seekers through their talks, which include the in-person testimonies of asylum seekers:

> One of the main principles of the gospel in Christ is that you cannot be disconnected from other people's suffering. Love connects with people's suffering. We go and make these presentations and the most powerful thing is the stories that these asylum seekers share. The program that we have has been very beautiful because the stories at these congregations have really touched people and have opened their eyes to their suffering but also to connect with someone that is seeking asylum. Similarly, at the synagogues when the asylum seekers share their stories, sometimes people approach you after the presentation and they talk about how painful it was that their family members were victims of the holocaust and suffer that horrible evil. Some of them cry when we're doing these presentations. And that's why they connect to helping and to walk in solidarity with asylum seekers.

Guillermo Torres describes this approach: "We're joining in solidarity with them, we're amplifying their voices of suffering and injustice. They have a voice."

Conclusion

Religious groups and congregations provide a venue for education outside of the channels of formal educational institutions. Most adults, particularly in marginalized communities, have little connection to formal educational institutions, nor the time and money to engage them.

Congregations, however, provide community members with opportunities several times a week to engage in ideas and apply them to their lives and surrounding neighborhoods. This makes congregations a valuable site for educating for social action in ways that are accessible for most adults.

The base community model, perhaps, shows most powerfully the potential of religious congregations for education and training people in marginalized communities for social change. The fact that base communities provide a venue for people, with or without a formal education or leadership position, to read and discuss sacred scriptures and then lead the efforts themselves to apply them to their local context shows the potential of religion for empowering people on the margins to lead movements to change the conditions that affect their lives.

The direct service model also shows the benefit of congregations as a site for community education. Congregations have physical space that can be used for educational events that many people feel comfortable and safe entering into. The Immigration Task Force's passport application events allowed undocumented parents to come to a space where they felt much safer and more welcome than a government office to learn how to protect their U.S. citizen children. The example of CLUE shows how Sunday services also provide a safe space for people to educate others by sharing their personal immigration stories and the ways in which they have been harmed by government policy. Most nonimmigrants have very few opportunities to hear these stories in any other context. Immigration then has the potential to become more than a political issue; it becomes a story about how fellow religious believers have experienced trauma and injustice.

Another benefit of religion in this educational project is providing persuasive language as to the importance of caring about marginalized immigrants. The ideas that every person is precious to God and therefore deserves certain rights and that those who are suffering are especially close to the heart of God are messages that have the power to persuade people of faith to engage the work of protecting immigrants or at least question their existing ideas about immigrants and immigration policy.

We also witnessed the power of religion in overcoming fear among immigrant leaders and rank-and-file believers in engaging in immigration protection work. Whether it is believers in a base community thinking of ways to resist unjust laws that affect their own lives or pastors wondering how to approach the controversial topic with their congregations, the idea that God is behind your efforts and will back you up in the face of backlash is a powerful antidote to fear. When people believe that God is behind them, they begin to fear less what mere humans and their governments can do to them.

We also witnessed the constraints that religion can place in the path of religious leaders and their followers who want to engage in the work of protecting and advocating for immigrants. We witnessed the influence of the dominant European American form of Christianity as creating obstacles for our case study organizations to educate people to protect and advocate for immigrants. Because of the legacy of complicity with European colonization and white supremacist ideas, most Christian congregations have a large contingent of members holding anti-immigrant views. Thus, any congregation, regardless of tradition, is going to face at least some resistance to educating for immigrant advocacy as a congregation. As we have seen, many immigrants themselves have adopted these anti-immigrant views as well. This makes educating congregations in the context of church services a risky proposition that has the potential to divide their congregations and, as Manny Arteaga experienced, lose a significant portion of their membership.

In the competitive U.S. religious marketplace, most pastors are dependent on their congregations for the financial support that provides their livelihoods. This makes any action on the part of pastors that threatens to anger even a small segment of their congregations financially risky, and angry members often leave their congregations for another of the plethora of options that the U.S. religious marketplace provides that better reflects their personal choices and values (Finke and Stark 1992).

The dominance of European American religious leaders also created obstacles for educating leaders even when those leaders were committed to the cause. The difficulties that Matthew 25 / Mateo 25 experienced with taking white leaders to the border and the tendency of white leaders to adopt a teaching and leading rather than learning posture made it difficult to teach white leaders the importance of letting immigrant leaders direct the movement.

Despite those constraints, educating leaders and believers about the realities of the immigration system and its deleterious effects on fellow believers draws on the deep resources of the very same religious cultures that create the obstacles. Paradoxically, the resources within religious cultures appear to have within them the tools to overcome the obstacles that the religious culture itself creates. Or conversely, the very same religious traditions that offer resources to educate people for advocacy contain within them the obstacles to successfully carrying out that task.

Conclusion

Faith

Religion has been used from the beginning of U.S. history to justify oppression. From the doctrine of discovery and manifest destiny justifying the theft and colonization of indigenous land (Charles and Rah 2019) to biblical justifications for slavery and Jim Crow (Kendi 2017; Emerson and Smith 2000; Tisby 2019; Baker 2017) and the current racist and anti-immigrant manifestations of Christian nationalism (Emerson and Bracey 2024; Whitehead and Perry 2020; Balmer 2021), Christianity has served in America to legitimate the oppression, exclusion, and marginalization of poor people, women, and people of color. Equally true is the fact that religion and spirituality, including Christianity, have been mobilized to resist these oppressions. Albeit in the minority, some religious leaders and institutions fueled the abolition movement, the civil rights movements of the 1960s, the labor movement, the women's rights movement, and, as we have seen, the immigrant rights movement (McAdam 1982; Morris 1984; Marsh 2006; Reed and Goldstein 2022).

Wood (2002) demonstrates that religion can and does act as both a resource and a constraint to contemporary social movements for change. Our analysis contributes to this discussion by demonstrating how faith can simultaneously enable and constrain the effectiveness of a social movement; we have explored the specific aspects of faith-based organizing that serve as unique advantages and unique obstacles to effectiveness in resisting oppression and promoting social change.

Our analysis has shown that faith-based organizations, particularly those led by Latinas/os, have played a significant role in current and past movements advocating for immigrants and immigration justice. Our historical summary has demonstrated that they have played this significant role at least since the first half of the twentieth century and that their role intensified beginning in the 1980s. Our case studies of the work of six Southern California faith-based organizations protecting immigrants during the Trump years and beyond revealed some of the unique ways that faith both enables and constrains the ability to effectively do this work. We discuss these enabling and constraining factors in this conclusion.

The Power of Religious Ideas and Symbols

It has been well established that religious ideas, practices, and symbols can provide motivation, clarity, hope, and endurance in movements seeking social reform (Wood 2002; Yukich 2013; Braunstein 2017; Diaz-Edelman 2017; Braunstein, Fuist, and Williams 2017). Max Weber (1978), in his seminal work on forms of authority, claims that charismatic authority, embodied in religious prophets and revolutionaries motivated by sacred ideals, can at certain times in history start movements that change the structures of society (Reed and Goldstein 2022). Sacred scriptures, narratives, and practices such as fasting, prayer vigils, hunger strikes, and communion rituals have also long been integrated into social movements to sustain and motivate the work (Lambelet 2019; Berryman 1984; Levine 1992; Braunstein 2017; Romero 2020). Core to this power of religion to motivate social change are ideas that humans are all one family created and loved by God and as such we are to love each other, that this is a higher law given by God that transcends human law, and that God is on the side of the oppressed. These ideas not only legitimate but also command believers to resist cooperating with unjust authorities in their harm of others and to work for justice.

We have seen in our cases the power of the use of religious ideas and symbols to motivate both grassroots advocates and powerful decision makers to work toward changing immigration policies and practices in the United States during a period of particularly harsh anti-immigrant rhetoric and enforcement policies. We saw several key religious concepts coming out of the biblical narrative that were consistently referenced:

1) God's command in the book of Leviticus 19 that "the foreigner residing among you must be treated as your native-born. Love them as yourself, for you were foreigners in Egypt."

2) The experience of Jesus's family as refugees fleeing state violence to Egypt soon after Jesus's birth.

3) Jesus's statement in Matthew 25 that "I was a stranger [immigrant] and you welcomed me," which directly implies that anyone who welcomes an immigrant welcomes him personally, and conversely anyone who excludes an immigrant excludes him.

We saw these references to ancient Jewish law and Jesus's life and teaching constantly in protest signs, in pleas to officials, and at speeches at trainings, rallies, and protests. Clearly, the participants in these actions were not simply motivated by an abstract universal principle that "every human life is important" but were connecting their activities in a very personal way to the sacred narratives of ancient Israel and the life of Jesus and thus seeing their participation as a way to personally serve and connect to a personal God. The concept that these narratives reinforce is the idea that God takes a special interest in the well-being of immigrants because of their vulnerable status and that to do harm to an immigrant is to do harm to God and to care for them is to find favor with God.

More broadly, we heard on numerous occasions in our interviews Rev. Martin Luther King Jr.'s concept of the "beloved community." As noted earlier, one leader told us, "Faith organizing by necessity is long term. Our goal is different. Our goal is the Kingdom of God, our goal is the beloved community." This goal of "building the Kingdom of God" or "the beloved community" transcends short-term policy goals. While secular organizing may be more effective at pursuing more targeted short-term policy goals, the more expansive goals of faith organizing have the potential to keep people motivated over longer periods and in the face of constant losses and disappointments. The belief that the Kingdom of God is going to grow and prevail in the end means that no effort is wasted and that short-term losses are no reason to despair or surrender. During the Trump administration there was little hope for large-scale policy reform, but faith leaders, many of whom had been pursuing immigration reform unsuccessfully for decades, were undaunted in continuing their work toward the "promised land." One longtime leader of one of our cases gave parallels between her life of activism and the narrative of Moses, who after forty years of leading the nation of Israel through the desert would not get to enter the promised land, but the next generation would get there. This confirms Yukich's (2013) conception of the New Sanctuary Movement as a multi-target social movement that seeks not only policy change but also the longer-term goal of changing their religious groups to live up to their call to embody love and justice for all. As noted, Yukich (2013) demonstrates that the multiple targets of a faith-based social movement often conflict with each other, sometimes making it less effective. Our analysis finds those same dynamics but also suggests that the multiple targets, particularly the long-term idealistic goal of bringing in the "beloved community" or "Kingdom of God," keep people engaged for the long haul in the face of repeated disappointment.

We also saw decision makers and politicians of faith respond to religious ideas and narratives that led them to change their minds. We heard from our interviews that appeals to the Jesuit Catholic faith of Governor Jerry Brown influenced him in supporting the Sanctuary State law SB54. We witnessed the power of appeals by Catholic leaders to key ICE officials in deciding on the release of particular individuals. We learned of the respect that two Baptist pastors had gained with Christian ICE and Border Patrol officers and how that often meant influence in advocating for particular individuals. We witnessed city council members change their minds on joining Attorney General Jeff Sessions's lawsuit opposing the Sanctuary State law through public appeals to their faith using scripture and religious language at city council meetings. We witnessed a Republican member of the House change her mind and sign on to a letter supporting DACA after meeting personally with faith leaders in her district.

In addition to the use of sacred ideas and narratives to influence decision makers in these movements, we saw many instances of embodied religious rituals being used in grassroots protests to inspire and sustain grassroots participants. We witnessed worship services, hunger strikes, and all-night prayer vigils in front of ICE headquarters in downtown Los Angeles. We witnessed public prayer and the reading of scripture at press conferences highlighting injustices in Trump's immigration policy. We witnessed rank-and-file church members fasting and praying for particular individuals detained by ICE to be released. The participants believed that these rituals have supernatural power to change the outcome of a particular case or policy, by drawing on the power of God to free the oppressed. It was also clear to us that these rituals brought personal strength, sustenance, and inspiration to the participants to keep going in the often discouraging and exhausting fight for change. The rituals provide a powerful link between the pressure campaign for changes in policy and a personal experience of the divine. This linkage makes a long-term commitment to advocating for immigration reform not just endurable but inspiring despite many disappointments.

Last, we demonstrated how religious ideals and symbols give courage to religious leaders and laypeople who have the most to lose in joining the movement for change—vulnerable immigrants themselves. We witnessed immigrant pastors through formal training at Fuller Seminary overcome their fear of engaging in the work of accompaniment and advocacy by hearing the testimonies of fellow pastors who overcame their fear by trusting in God. We witnessed a vulnerable undocumented pastor, Luis Reyes, being willing to become the public face of a national campaign to resist President Trump's enforcement regime at great cost to his and his family's privacy because of his faith in God. We witnessed undocumented believers willing to speak publicly in front of congregations composed mostly of nonimmigrants telling their traumatic stories at great risk to themselves and their families. All of this courage was enhanced by their conviction that God was behind them and would be with them even if hardship ensued as a result of their activism.

All of this suggests that religious ideas and symbols have power to inspire people to both take risks in the face of danger and endure in the face of disappointment. It also suggests that they have the power to change the perspective of those in power to the point of changing their mind on policy decisions.

Faith-Based Organizations as Bridging Institutions

Social capital is defined in the sociological literature as "the ability of actors to secure benefits by virtue of membership in social networks or other social structures" (Portes 1998, 6). Those in positions of power have access to relationships with other powerful people whom they can activate to help realize their goals, whether economic, political, or social (Portes 1998; Bourdieu 1997). Social capital tends to be concentrated among the privileged members of society and weak among those on the margins who lack access to people in positions to help them realize their objectives. Therefore, relational connections serve to reproduce the inequalities of power, wealth, and status in a society (Bourdieu 1997). Putnam (2000) makes the distinction between bonding and bridging social capital—the latter referring to connections across social divides and inequalities based on race, class, and political power. Bridging social capital is key for disempowered groups in society because it allows for the broadening of relationships that can provide access to people with more resources and power to pursue their goals.

Wood (2002, 267) makes the case that faith-based organizations can serve as bridging institutions, connecting people to political power who would otherwise be shut out of the political process. "On the basis of the more extensive social capital embedded in religious institutions, faith-based organizing is able to achieve a more influential role in city and state politics, as what I termed bridging institutions in the public realm, linking civil society upward to the political society and the state." He goes on to say that these faith-based organizations are crucial for democratic reform in the United States because they "draw on some of the richest of American cultural traditions—volunteerism, citizen activism, and often religiously inspired work for democratic reform" (Wood 2002, 267).

We see this bridging function in our analysis of case studies in a number of ways. First of all, our organizations connected vulnerable immigrants with more resourced congregation members through accompaniment work. Through these organizations, asylum seekers, detainees, and their families become personally connected to individuals they would otherwise never have met who could provide access to housing, basic needs, jobs, transportation, and legal support. As we have demonstrated, religious organizations are particularly rich sources of people motivated by their faith traditions to personally care for people who are suffering and vulnerable.

Second, these faith-based organizations can then connect these volunteers and vulnerable immigrants to grassroots organizers who give them access to decision makers through advocacy campaigns for policy change. These organizers link members together with others who are passionate for policy change and give them strategies for social/structural change that they would not otherwise have access to. Motivated by the injustices they have either experienced or witnessed, congregation members and religious believers now have the ability to channel their passion into grassroots political action. Most U.S. residents are unaware of how laws, policies, and practices are created and implemented—and how they can be influenced. Their primary connection to the political system is through voting for representatives who are then supposed to represent the will of the voters who elected them. In reality, most policy is influenced by powerful interest groups funding the campaigns of and lobbying representatives (Gilens and Page 2014; Domhoff 2013). The faith-based organizations we studied connect congregation members who have no experience in the world of political organizing (and who are probably unlikely to join secular advocacy groups) to decision makers through grassroots campaigns, thus bridging, as Wood (2002) describes, civil society to the state. We witnessed faith leaders connecting undocumented young people, for example, with top officials who influence the policies that affect their lives, telling their stories and speaking truth to power.

Last, our organizations bridge community organizers to powerful decision makers of faith through "grasstops" relationships. As we have seen, secular advocacy organizations often do not have personal relationships with decision makers and in some cases have an adversarial relationship with them because of the nature of their advocacy work. Faith leaders can sometimes bridge the divide between grassroots organizers who have the same policy reform goals and decision makers who have the same faith commitments. As discussed with the case of advocacy for the Sanctuary State bill (SB54), Fr. Brendan Busse provided a personal bridge to Governor Jerry Brown, who shared his Jesuit faith, young women who were separated from their families by ICE who attended their church in East LA, and grassroots secular immigrant rights organizers pushing for the law. Matthew 25 / Mateo 25, CLUE, LA Voice, the Catholic Church, and other organizations had ongoing "ministerial" and "discipleship" relationships with ICE officials, members of Congress, and other decision makers that appear to have influenced them at different times in key decisions.

Religious and Spiritual Practice as Cultural Community Wealth

In addition to serving as bridging institutions and providing inspiring ideas and symbols, religion and spirituality can be seen as a source of cultural community wealth (CCW) within immigrant communities that can be leveraged to resist oppression (Park, Dizon, and Malcolm 2019). The conception of CCW is a response from critical race theory to Bourdieu's construct of cultural capital. Bourdieu and Passeron (1977) refer to cultural capital as the knowledge, skills, mannerisms, and tastes that allow one to advance in society. Cultural capital, therefore, reproduces class inequalities as it functions to limit those from lower classes from accessing certain opportunities and resources. From this perspective, working-class groups and communities of color lack the cultural capital to help them advance in society. Yosso (2005) challenged the assumption in this theory that communities of color are lacking in cultural resources to resist their oppression and advance in society.

Yosso (2005) categorizes the sources of CCW that communities of color possess to overcome obstacles and resist the forces that marginalize them: aspirational, familial, resistant, linguistic, social, and navigational capital (Park, Dizon, and Malcolm 2019). Pérez Huber (2009, 721), in her study of undocumented Chicana students, added a seventh category of CCW—*spiritual capital*, which she defines as "a set of resources and skills rooted in a spiritual connection to a reality greater than oneself." She demonstrates that religious beliefs and spirituality serve as sources of resilience in the form of faith and hope to persevere in the face of obstacles.

Park, Dizon, and Malcolm (2019) demonstrate how spiritual capital supports the different forms of CCW identified by Yosso (2005). In our cases, we witnessed how spiritual capital energizes what Yosso calls resistant capital—the capacity to challenge social norms and inequalities through oppositional behavior and/or transformative actions. This also includes challenging assumptions of cultural inferiority and encouraging actions of resistance (Park, Dizon, and Malcolm 2019).

This spiritual capital was evident in our observations of Latina/o religious believers gathering outside of ICE headquarters engaged in a weeklong hunger strike, calling on ICE to release two pastors from Adelanto detention facility. On other occasions we witnessed religious believers blocking with their bodies buses that were chartered by ICE to transport detainees from an ICE detention facility in downtown Los Angeles to Adelanto, chanting, "No estan solo." All of these events were led by and consisted of mostly Latina/o immigrant religious leaders and their congregants, challenging the narrative of a powerless, timid, and culturally inferior minority. The courage and motivation to carry out these acts of resistance, despite all of the incentives, religious and otherwise, to stay silent, were encouraged and fueled by the religious faith of the participants and embedded in religious symbols, language, prayers, and worship music.

The base community model as practiced by Rev. Toña Rios at Baldwin Park United Methodist Church and by Fr. Brenden Busse at Dolores Mission in East Los Angeles shows how a seemingly simple act of gathering a group of twenty people together for a Bible study to read the teachings of Jesus, to share their personal struggles and ask the question, "How do we apply this in our own neighborhood?" can be a powerful act of resistance (see Salvatierra and Wrencher 2022). As the base community at Rev. Rios's church shared how their lives and the lives of their neighbors were being seriously disrupted by the racial profiling and impounding of cars by the police in their community, they decided to apply the teachings of their faith to stand up to a government entity much more powerful than themselves, at great risk to themselves, and succeeded in changing an oppressive policy.

These examples show the power of religion to inspire acts of resistance against forces much more powerful, at least according to appearances, than themselves. Yet the power of their religious and spiritual practices, in some cases, proved to be a force more powerful than that of the state authorities. As Pérez Huber (2009) and Park, Dizon, and Malcolm (2019) demonstrate, the power of religious and spiritual practices and language must not be neglected as a force for social change.

Constraints

While our analysis has clearly shown that faith can enable social movements on behalf of a marginalized group, it can also simultaneously act as a constraint on effective action for social change. Wood (2002), in his study of the national PICO network, concludes that "religious cultures" can both enable and constrain social movements. Often the constraints come from particular religious cultures that create obstacles to cooperation with organizations and leaders of other faiths or racial/ethnic groups. In our cases, we clearly witnessed both the enabling power of "religious cultures" in fueling a social movement as well as constraints. We have identified three primary constraints in our cases coming from the faith-based organizations we analyzed (1) the legacy of the dominance of Euro-American forms of Christianity, (2) religious orientations toward submitting to authority, and (3) the multi-target nature of faith-based organizing.

The Dominance of Euro-American Christianity

The most dominant religious organizations in the United States are those associated with Euro-American Christianity. While there has been much written about the increased percentage of U.S. residents not identifying with any religion, and the decline of religious attendance, 71 percent of people in the United States still identify as Christian, and 34 percent attended a Christian church at least once a month in 2021 (National Opinion Research Center 2021). The most dominant religious groups in America can be divided into roughly three groups: Catholic, mainline Protestant, and evangelical Protestant. Of U.S. residents, 21 percent identify themselves as Catholic, 25 percent as evangelical Protestant, and 15 percent as mainline Protestant.

While members of the three dominant forms of U.S. Christianity are increasingly racially and ethnically diverse, the institutions of all three of these Christian groups have been and still are dominated by European Americans and shaped by the historical dominance of Euro-American Christianity in the United States. The majority of the institutions of all three historically supported the displacement of Native Americans, the doctrine of discovery, and manifest destiny (Kendi 2017; Charles and Rah 2019; Romero 2020). As a result, the dominant institutions of U.S. Christianity, established and controlled by immigrants from Europe and their descendants, have for most of their history supported and legitimated the idea of the United States as a predominantly white nation (Kendi 2017; Baker 2017; Charles and Rah 2019). Thus, the debates in U.S. society around immigration, whether in secular or religious contexts, take for granted that the current U.S. boundaries and the dominance of a European American majority are legitimate and uncontested. The main question centered around immigration in the dominant cultural discourse is this: "Is immigration from (mostly nonwhite) nations good for U.S. 'native-born' (mostly white) citizens?" rather than "Do we, as descendants of immigrants who violently displaced those who lived here for centuries, have any right to forbid others from living here?" or even "Do we, as the descendants of those who stole land from native people, have the right to live here?" The European American dominance of Christian institutions in America reinforces the uncontested idea that the current borders that exist are legitimate and the mostly white descendants of those who immigrated here in past centuries have a God-given right to control those borders according to whether or not it benefits them.

In addition to reinforcing these assumptions, a growing body of research shows that the more white people identify with the Christian religion, the more likely they are to oppose immigration and think that immigrants are harmful to the United States (Melkonian-Hoover and Kellstedt 2019; Emerson and Bracey 2024). This empirical evidence clearly shows that connection to the dominant institutions of Christianity in the United States on average reinforces anti-immigrant ideas and policies. This makes it difficult to organize a movement for immigration justice within those institutions.

In our research, we witnessed this as a powerful constraint. On the one hand, as we have seen, in predominantly white congregations, across the spectrum of mainline, evangelical, and Catholic, pastors and priests believe it is controversial to advocate openly for immigrants from the pulpit during a Sunday morning service because they know that a significant number of their members hold anti-immigrant views. In addition, immigrant leaders of predominantly immigrant congregations also reported that advocating for immigrants was controversial within their congregations, as some had adopted anti-immigrant sentiments from white leaders within their tradition or from the dominant culture at large. In addition, immigrants with legal status were sometimes prone to judge their undocumented brethren, citing the biblical mandate to obey the law, making it difficult for the leaders of those congregations to advocate for them openly.

In the U.S. religious economy, in which participation is voluntary and churches compete with each other for memberships and donations, most pastors feel that they cannot afford to alienate members who help pay their bills with controversial political positions (Finke and Stark 1992).

This difficulty was exacerbated by the Trump presidency, which brought extreme anti-immigrant rhetoric, coupled with statements purportedly supporting "Christian values" to the forefront of U.S. politics. In addition, Latina/o leaders and their congregations are often very influenced by the dominant white leaders in their denominations and often adopt their anti-immigrant sentiments, even as some or most of their congregations are recent immigrants. We witnessed a number of Latina/o pastors leading mostly immigrant Latina/o churches actively opposing policies for immigration reform and in some cases even demanding of their local representatives that they do more to stop the flow of "illegals" into the United States.

Within white Protestant institutions, the historic conflict between more progressive white mainline, and more conservative evangelical denominations and leaders creates an additional layer of barriers to organizing a movement for immigration justice across racial and denominational lines. U.S. Protestantism is unique in the world as having experienced what became known as the fundamentalist/modernist split around the turn of the twentieth century. The split began with a debate within the U.S. Presbyterian denomination over the ideas of higher criticism of the Bible that had become popular in Germany (Longfield 1991; Marsden 2006). This led to a countermovement, later called fundamentalism, that reaffirmed belief in the Bible as inerrant and inspired by God. While the split began over interpretations of the Bible, the two sides later split over the so-called social gospel as well, with fundamentalists claiming that preaching the gospel of individual salvation through the atonement of Jesus should take precedence over attempts to reform society to become more just and equal (Moberg 2006; Marsden 2006). By the middle of the twentieth century, most Protestant denominations (Presbyterian, Methodist, Episcopalian, Lutheran) had sided with the modernist interpretation of the Bible and supported efforts to reform society, while the fundamentalist movement created their own Bible colleges (Biola, Moody), seminaries (Dallas, Fuller), and publishing houses (Zondervan). The Southern Baptist, Missouri Synod Lutheran, and Pentecostal Assemblies of God and Foursquare denominations largely adopted the fundamentalist perspective. Interestingly, the separate African American Christian denominations did not undergo this fundamentalist/modernist split.

This historical split in white Protestantism complicates the ability to organize a movement for immigration justice within the institutions of U.S. Christianity. On the one hand, the official leadership of most of the mainline Protestant denominations have taken strong pro-immigrant stances and have advocated for comprehensive immigration reform. However, the largest, youngest, and fastest growing Protestant congregations, including among immigrants, are within the evangelical and Pentecostal traditions that, because of the historic split with mainline denominations, tend to eschew efforts for social reform in favor of focusing on personal evangelism (Mulder, Ramos, and Marti 2017). To the extent they are involved in politics, they tend to emphasize conservative positions on abortion, gay marriage, and religious liberty (Mulder, Ramos, and Marti 2017) rather than more progressive stances on immigrant rights, antiracism, antisexism, and economic equality. In addition, the fastest growing Latina/o congregations are in the Pentecostal (including Assemblies of God and Foursquare) or evangelical traditions (Martinez 2018; Espinosa 2016; Pew Research Center 2014). Most of the immigrant leaders and leaders of color in these congregations have been influenced by the white leadership of these conservative denominations that prioritize the individual salvation that comes from the atonement of Jesus on the cross rather than social reform. To the extent that these denominations do address political issues, they tend to focus on the Republican-friendly issues of abortion, gay marriage, and religious liberty. There are exceptions, however. Most notably, national Assemblies of God leaders Jesse Miranda and Samuel Rodriguez invested heavily in efforts to promote immigration reform during the Bush and Obama administrations, mobilizing Latino Pentecostal leaders to advocate for comprehensive immigration reform (Martinez 2018; Espinosa 2016). Rodriguez continued to promote immigration justice as a priority during the Trump presidency, even though he supported the president and became his close advisor because of his positions on abortion, religious freedom, and same-sex marriage. Most mainline Protestant congregations, on the other hand, which are more progressive politically, are more likely to be in numerical decline and remain predominantly white and older.

Thus, the legacy of the white Protestant fundamentalist/modernist split makes it more difficult to mobilize immigrant congregations for

immigration reform because the fastest growing immigrant congregations have emerged through the traditions of the fundamentalist side
of this split in which social reform is seen as a distraction from the gospel of individual salvation in Jesus. The white Protestant denominations
that are most motivated to pursue immigration reform because of their
theological emphasis on social reform are the least likely to contain immigrant members and leaders. The white leaders from these denominations often use theological terms and political rhetoric that are alienating
to immigrant evangelical leaders. Thus, the divisions within white Protestantism have prevented a unified response among immigrant religious
leaders to issues of immigration justice.

Another theme that emerged in all of our cases was the difficulty of
combining white-led organizations, congregations, and denominations
with immigrant pastors and organizational leaders in doing the work
of protecting immigrants. In particular, the culturally specific ways in
which white-led organizations do their work, with more protocol, bureaucratic structures, and formally democratic processes, often clashed
with the ways in which immigrant-led congregations and organizations
operate, with less rigid rules, boundaries, and organizational structures
and with more deference given to leaders. While these differences in the
culture of how organizations operate are not surprising, they are difficult to overcome because white-led organizations, congregations, and
denominations often had more influence, resources, and an expectation, whether explicit or implicit, of being the ones to decide how things
would be done.

This discovery aligns with other researchers (Cobb, Perry, and
Dougherty 2015; Dougherty and Huyser 2008; Edwards 2008; Edwards,
Christerson, and Emerson 2013) who have found that in multiracial religious organizations that include white people, white culture and leadership is typically elevated as the default because that is the norm in the
wider society and is an expectation among white members and leaders.

Despite these obstacles, we did see a significant number of Latina/o
evangelical leaders and congregations willing to advocate for immigrants
and for immigration reform. Organizations like Matthew 25 / Mateo 25,
CLUE, and We Care are engaged in empowering Latina/o evangelical
leaders to break out of the constraints of the white-dominant institu-

tional field of Protestant Christianity in the United States that has been configured by the fundamentalist/modernist split. There has always been and continues to be a group of Latina/o evangelical leaders who represent a perspective that is different from both conservative evangelical and more progressive mainline Protestantism (Romero 2020). A uniquely Latina/o Protestantism exists that, similar to many Black Protestant traditions, combines the view of the Bible as the inspired word of God and the importance of a personal relationship with God through the death and resurrection of Jesus with the centrality of working for justice in the living out of the Christian faith (Espinosa 2016; Mulder, Ramos, and Marti 2017). The political orientation of these leaders seems to be different from those of either white conservative evangelicals or white mainline progressives. They tend to be pro–labor rights, pro–economic safety net, and pro–immigration reform, but also pro-life, pro–religious liberty (as defined by white evangelicals), and anti–gay marriage (Mulder, Ramos, and Marti 2017). There is a new generation of young evangelical leaders, however, who are critical of their parents' generation on the issue of LGBTQ rights. Thus, we saw evidence in our cases of a uniquely Latina/o Protestantism that does not neatly fit into the evangelical/mainline duality of white Protestantism in America.

The United Methodist Church's Welcoming Congregations initiative is an interesting attempt to build up the voices of a new generation of Latina/o leaders who are not bound by the white fundamentalist/ modernist split in their perspective. They have prioritized hiring young Latina/o pastors, many of whom come from evangelical backgrounds but want to incorporate social action with their ministries. However, this attempt has not been without its challenges. Because of the strong institutional bureaucracy of the Methodist Church, the Latina/o leaders recruited to do the work of advocacy still have to navigate not only the progressive theological and political culture of white Methodism but also the organizational culture. Some of the Latino leaders of welcoming congregations whom we interviewed spoke of the burdensome meetings, reports, and proposals that they must submit in order to be part of the Methodist institutional infrastructure. This seemed completely foreign to them based on their experience in Latina/o congregations, where there is much greater flexibility given to the pastor and where agreements and decisions arise out of informal relationships rather than bureaucratic structures. They felt that formal meetings, written reports, and proposals took up a significant amount of time that could be used to do the work that they were hired to do, and feel called to do—serving and advocating for their neighbors. Similarly, *puentes* and Latina/o leaders involved in Matthew 25 / Mateo 25 described the frustrations of the Latina/o leaders in partnership with predominantly white churches coming from what seemed to them to be endless meetings and delays coming from the highly structured approval process of predominantly white congregations. In addition, there seemed to be an expectation that the organizational norms of the white leaders were to be followed by the group if the white leaders were to be involved.

Our cases used various strategies to try to overcome the obstacles articulated above. We Care, for example, is a Latina/o immigrant-led organization that functions according to the strength of the networks of mostly Latina/o leaders connected to the founding pastors. To the extent that white leaders and institutions are involved in their work, it is through responding to a specific need that is sent out through the pastors' network—but the pastors are clearly directing the efforts. Thus, We Care avoids some of the problems arising from white dominance through its network, rather than bureaucratic governance structure. Matthew 25 / Mateo 25 has prioritized Latina/o leadership in its partnerships, but central to its vision is the partnership of immigrant and nonimmigrant churches to "change the hearts and minds" of white Christians to support immigration reform. This has proven to be difficult and complicated work that has led to high turnover of leaders and congregations engaging in the work. Their use of bicultural young *puentes* to negotiate the difficulties of combining predominantly white congregations with immigrant congregations is their primary strategy.

The various configurations of the work of the Catholic Church focus mostly on immigrant congregations and base communities in immigrant neighborhoods doing the work so as to avoid the controversies that come from engaging a wider swath of majority-white Catholicism. LA Voice avoids the clash of religious cultures by focusing its immigration work on partnerships with individual mainline and Catholic congregations, most of whom are in immigrant neighborhoods led by pastors already committed to the cause. CLUE strategically hired Guillermo Torres to bring Latina/o evangelical leaders and mainline Protestants, Jews, and Muslims together to do immigration advocacy. He is uniquely situated to do this work because he has ties to both mainline and evangelical immigrant congregations, but there are tensions in bringing together such a wide spectrum of theological and political orientations to the work.

Thus, the historic domination of Euro-American Christianity in the U.S. religious landscape creates obstacles and complications to organizing an immigrant-led movement for immigration justice within the institutional structures of faith-based organizations. While our cases tried to overcome these obstacles in different ways, they remain significant complicating factors to a more unified faith-based movement.

Faith-Based Organizing as a Multi-target Social Movement

As we saw, in her analysis of the New Sanctuary Movement in the late 2000s, Yukich (2013) identifies what she calls a multi-target social movement (MTSM). She defines an MTSM as "a movement or movement organization that simultaneously seeks change in more than one arena." She concludes the following about the New Sanctuary Movement: "In mobilizing religious communities, their aims went beyond the common movement strategy of organizing congregations to create a broader activist base for social and political change. This was part of New Sanctuary's endgame but it was not the sole part. Instead, they also sought to mobilize religious congregations in order to challenge dominant, largely conservative, religious authority in the United States and to transform the religious and spiritual lives of those involved, moving them toward a more progressive, global, inclusive religious vision" (10). While she makes the case that MTSMs have the potential for greater degrees of social change than single-target movements, she identifies the difficulties of pursuing more than one goal as a movement. Having more than one goal means that "the process of strategy selection in multi-target social movements will be longer and more contested than in other movements or movement organizations, since fewer crossover strategies exist" (211).

Our cases, for the most part, fit into Yukich's (2013) conception of faith-based efforts to protect immigrants as an MTSM. These organizations not only had specific policy goals (passing the Sanctuary State bill, advocating for the release of detainees during the COVID-19 pandemic, etc.) but also had broader religious goals, such as unifying immigrant and nonimmigrant believers, expanding the view of God's vision of the church to include advocacy for justice, and ultimately growing the "Kingdom of God" or the "beloved community"—a vision of a just and equal society based on love where everyone has the ability to thrive. While these larger goals, as we noted previously, keep leaders and participants motivated over the long term, even in the face of discouraging defeats, they also can constrain the ability to organize for more practical short-term goals.

In the case of Matthew 25 / Mateo 25, for example, the leadership sees accompaniment work as a means to unite immigrant and nonimmigrant Christian believers in protecting those most vulnerable. The ultimate goal for this union is not only getting nonimmigrant congregational support for immigration reform but more broadly unifying the church across current racial/ethnic divides. Having these multiple targets makes strategizing more difficult and time-consuming. Matthew 25 / Mateo 25 has evolved more slowly and deliberately in its strategies compared to secular single-target organizations which focus only on winning specific policy goals, or compared to single-target groups like We Care, which focus mostly on accompaniment goals. Its goal of pairing immigrant and nonimmigrant congregations to form support circles and thus unify under the common goal of protecting vulnerable immigrants has led to painstaking strategies of meeting together, worshiping together, and training a cadre of *puentes* to translate differences and negotiate conflict. All of this meeting, peacemaking, and strategizing requires an enormous investment of time and emotional energy, which some argue seems to get in the way of doing the practical work of accompaniment and advocacy. It has also led some to question whether it would be easier and more efficient to recruit exclusively immigrant congregations to do the work of accompaniment and advocacy and has led to a turnover of congregations that have cycled in and out of support circles as some have become frustrated with this strategy of partnering immigrant and nonimmigrant congregations. However, the leaders of Matthew 25 / Mateo 25 believe that the larger goal of immigration reform will not be possible if white nonimmigrant congregations are not mobilized since they constitute the bulk of the resistance to immigration reform in the

United States. Time will tell whether Matthew 25 / Mateo 25 will succeed in its ultimate goal of influencing Congress by enlisting nonimmigrant churches in the fight for immigration reform and in the process changing the views of white Christians in the United States toward a more just and welcoming immigration policy. The ambitious long-term goal, however, makes short-term goals more difficult to achieve.

The case of the UMC's Welcoming Congregations initiative can be seen as a local version of an MTSM. The goals of this project are to serve their immigrant communities in whatever capacities are needed, which have come to include legal assistance, trauma care, food provision, youth leadership development, and political organizing for state and local political change, all of this in addition to ministering to the spiritual needs of their communities. This initiative, however, is simpler than that of Matthew 25 / Mateo 25 because it exists within a single bureaucracy and is focused on specific locations. Their leadership comes completely from within the UMC denomination and therefore is subject to less difficulty in mobilizing a wide array of leaders from multiple traditions. Thus, while the UMC initiative has a wider array of targets than We Care, it is more restricted in its focus compared to Matthew 25 / Mateo 25. Conflict regarding strategy and organization seems to come more from cultural differences within the organization as opposed to between multiple targets within the organization.

CLUE and LA Voice are also organizations with multiple targets. Not only is immigration reform only one of the multiple political goals they are pursuing, which include supporting organized labor campaigns, criminal justice reform, and housing policy, but they are also multifaith organizations. Working with leaders of Muslims, Jews, and Christians under the banner of pursuing a more just society complicates their mission even further. In both cases, their strategy related to immigration is to work primarily with leaders and congregations that are already committed to promoting immigration reform, which tends to be predominantly immigrant congregations and white progressive Jewish and mainline Protestant congregations. LA Voice deals with the complications of multiple goals, multiple faiths, and multiple constituencies by allowing each individual congregation to decide what advocacy campaigns fit best with their interests and works to support them in their goals. This leads to a wide constellation of efforts and projects supported by LA Voice and limits the conflict that comes from trying to bring together different traditions and religious cultures in a single campaign. But it also limits the ability to mobilize around a single issue like immigration.

Overall, our cases provide support for Yukich's (2013) conclusion that faith-based organizing to protect vulnerable immigrants tends to combine multiple goals that often complicate the ability to achieve short-term goals. Yet at the same time, the transcendent nature of some of those multiple goals, including building the Kingdom of God and/or the "beloved community," can serve to motivate people over long periods in the face of discouraging losses.

Religion and Obedience to Authority

Finally, and perhaps more fundamentally, a constraint of faith-based organizing to challenge government policies and practices is the emphasis of most religions on obedience to authority. While most religions conceive of a "higher law" that takes precedence over human laws when they conflict, most religions also encourage obedience to laws and authorities in most cases. In addition, most religious congregations and organizations are organized hierarchically, with pastors, priests, rabbis, and imams providing authoritative teachings on how members live out their faith, and typically as a result have the strongest voice in decisions made by the congregation, even if formally a board of elders or members are technically in charge of decisions. While most religions, and certainly those dominant in the United States, have strong theologies and traditions to draw upon to resist unjust laws and authorities, the religious cultures of most congregations are oriented toward conforming to authorities, whether secular or religious. This makes the work of resistance, which may include confrontation with authorities and breaking laws, uncomfortable for most religious believers.

Wood (2002, 278) identifies this constraint: "All of the religious traditions present within this kind of democratic organizing include prophetic dimensions, and in most of them this prophetic tradition remains salient enough to undergird and make sense of the conflict inherent in civic engagement. But in the United States, at least, most also have sufficiently internalized standards of 'polite' Christianity and/or religious teachings of obeisance to authority and public conflict often sits uncomfortably and feels vaguely un-Christian." We saw this discomfort manifest itself in the reluctance of Latina/o religious leaders and their followers to engage in advocacy to resist or change laws. This was particularly true among evangelical pastors who come from traditions influenced by Euro-American evangelicalism, which emphasizes submission to authority, obeying the law, and focusing on individual salvation rather than on social change. We also witnessed a sense of shame among undocumented believers because of their status; they are defined by the surrounding society as lawbreakers, constraining their willingness to engage in active resistance or even to talk about their status with fellow believers. In addition, their documented fellow believers often do not have a positive view of them for the same reason. This produced a reluctance among those who would benefit the most from policy and enforcement changes to address the issue for fear of being "outed" in their congregations.

We also witnessed a hesitancy among religious leaders, even when willing to engage in advocacy, to join with secular organizations in more confrontational actions with authorities. They preferred a more polite, friendly, and nonconfrontational approach. While this hesitancy acts as a constraint in pressuring authorities to change policies and practices, we also saw this in some cases operate as an advantage in gaining access to decision makers. Some of the faith leaders we interviewed expressed that decision makers would rather meet with them than with their secular counterparts because of their more friendly, less confrontational approach. It could be that both confrontational and polite, friendly appeals to decision makers are needed and that faith-based movements are uniquely positioned and more comfortable playing the more friendly role. Wood (2002, 279) also recognized this as a potential contribution of faith-based advocacy: "While in some sense a limitation, this emphasis on dialogue may foster political partnership, institutional influence, and concrete reform. By leading away from polarization and attack as the dominant modus operandi of contemporary politics, and by organizing marginalized groups to exercise political power, it may also contribute to building an American polity that is both more civil and more democratic." We witnessed that polite, friendly dialogue, particularly with decision makers who share the same faith, can be effective as a strategy to, as one faith leader told us, "become an ally of the part of them that wants something more—that wants what God wants, that wants the common good." We witnessed, for example, the pastors/leaders of We Care leveraging their status as pastors along with respect and politeness with ICE authorities to gain access to and influence individual cases of detainees.

We also witnessed, however, this politeness and desire to submit to authority limiting the willingness of leaders and congregation members to engage in actions pushing for change. We witnessed immigrant leaders in evangelical congregations adopting the anti-immigrant "law-and-order" rhetoric of the white leaders of their denominations and traditions. We witnessed this hesitancy of their elder faith leaders to more directly confront authorities and their unjust policies and practices, leading to frustration among young people in Latina/o congregations. In some congregations this has created a generational divide that is splitting their congregations as young people, hungry to see changes to the laws that have traumatized their families, are leaving their churches to find support for a more prophetic and confrontational activism.

Conclusion: The Power and Constraints of Faith-Based Social Movements

While early social theorists such as Marx and Durkheim conceptualized religion for the most part as a legitimator of authority and the status quo, others such as Weber, while mostly concurring, also saw the potential of religion for social change at certain times in history. A number of contemporary scholars of social change have demonstrated this potential in current movements for change (see, e.g., Braunstein 2017; Wood 2002; Braunstein, Fuist, and Williams 2017; Reed and Goldstein 2022). Our analysis has taken the case of faith-based organizations working to defend and advocate for immigrants at a time of strong anti-immigrant sentiment among white practicing Christians and a federal administration increasing the use of harsh anti-immigrant rhetoric and aggressive enforcement measures. It has provided significant evidence of the power of religion to motivate people through appeals to the higher power of a transcendent God, to provide bridging institutions to connect people to social movements who would otherwise not likely engage, and to be a resource of cultural community wealth in marginalized communities to resist the forces that oppress them.

We also uncovered evidence of the ways in which religion constrains movements for change. Perhaps most significantly, we found the institutional, theological, and cultural dominance of European American forms of Christianity as a significant constraint to the mobilization of Latina/o leaders and believers in challenging the systems that limit, marginalize, and traumatize immigrant families. And we witnessed how the multiple targets of faith-based organizing can undermine effectiveness, even as they bring sustenance for the long fight for change.

What is clear from our analysis, however, is that faith-based organizing brings *unique* contributions, which when combined with secular movements and organizations can add to the collective power of social movements for change. Understanding both the unique contributions and the unique constraints of faith-based organizing for change is crucial for theorists and practitioners of faith who are working for a different and better world than the one we live in. In particular, the religious faith of marginalized communities, *if they can apply their own theologies and approaches to social action apart from the religious cultures of dominant European American religious institutions*, is a rich source of cultural community wealth to resist the harms imposed on them by the policies and practices of the dominant society in which they reside.

ACKNOWLEDGMENTS

This book exists only because of the thousands of immigrant and non-immigrant servants of God who daily pour out their sweat, blood, and tears toward the dream of immigrant justice. We hope and pray that this book will help bring visibility to your *obra* (work).

The book grew out of our friendship and collaboration together in the movement to accompany, defend, and advocate for vulnerable people whose lives are uprooted and often traumatized by violence, poverty, and abuse by governments. We would like to thank first and foremost those people willing to share their migration stories with us. We understand that these are not easy things to share openly. We sincerely hope that we have conveyed these experiences accurately and compassionately, and that the telling of these stories will contribute somehow to a more just, compassionate, and loving world. We would also like to thank the many faith leaders, activists, clergy, lay leaders, and volunteers who are willing to give so much of their lives in the hope that a better world is possible. We would like to thank them for their many hours spent answering our questions and openly sharing their stories of success, failure, frustration, conflict, joy, and hope. We value those hours they spent with us because we know how much time and energy they spend in their work for justice.

We would also like to thank the many research assistants who helped us conduct this research. Special thanks to Jenny Velasco, Fernando Villegas, Fernanda Soto, and Luisa Ortez for your fantastic interviewing and translation skills, and to Katelyn Steele and Naomi Welikala for your excellent work translating some of our transcriptions. Thanks to Clarissa Brunt for organizing the transcription of our interviews in multiple languages.

We thank Jennifer Hammer for her supportive and helpful editorial comments. Last, we would like to thank Dr. Edwin Aponte, Don Richter, and the Louisville Institute for funding the project and believing in its potential.

NOTES

1. HISTORY

1 Names of key leaders have been changed.

2. CONTEXT

1 The labor movement as a whole underwent a major shift in the mid-twentieth century from advocacy for more restrictive immigration policies to advocacy for more liberal policies, largely as major labor leaders prioritized new organizing of immigrant workers over the protection of existing jobs. The AFL-CIO now formally supports comprehensive immigration reform. However, only the most progressive labor unions are actively involved in immigration organizing and ongoing advocacy.

2 "All popes tend to have a couple of catchphrases they invoke time after time, so after a while they come to sum up a whole chunk of his thought. 'Be not afraid!' was such a phrase for John Paul II, and 'reason and faith' for Benedict XVI. It's becoming steadily clearer that for Francis, perhaps his core signature phrase is the 'culture of encounter'" (Allen 2013).

3 Exhibition catalogue, Andy Warhol's first international retrospective exhibition at the Moderna Museet gallery in Stockholm (February 1968).

4 Melkonian-Hoover and Kellstedt (2019) analyzed survey data from the best sources available, including Gallup polls, the General Social Survey (GSS), American National Election Surveys, the Pew Religion Landscape Survey, the Public Religion Research Institute, and the Henry Institute's Cooperative Clergy Survey.

3. ACCOMPANIMENT

1 Names of asylum seekers have been changed to protect privacy.
2 Names have been changed to protect privacy.

4. ADVOCACY

1 Names have been changed to protect privacy.

BIBLIOGRAPHY

Allen, John L., Jr. 2013. "Francis and the 'Culture of Encounter.'" *National Catholic Reporter*, December 20. www.ncronline.org.

Baker, Kelly J. 2017. *Gospel According to the Klan: The KKK's Appeal to Protestant America, 1915–1930*. Lawrence: University Press of Kansas.

Balmer, Randall. 2021. *Bad Faith: Race and the Rise of the Religious Right*. Grand Rapids, MI: Eerdmans.

Barba, Lloyd D., and Tatyana Castillo-Ramos. 2019. "Sacred Resistance: The Sanctuary Movement from Reagan to Trump." *Perspectivas* 16:11–36.

———. 2021. "Latinx Leadership and Legacies in the US Sanctuary Movement, 1980–2020." *American Religion* 3(1):1–24.

Barreto, Matt A., Sylvia Manzano, Ricardo Ramirez, and Kathy Rim. 2009. "Mobilization, Participation, and Solidaridad: Latino Participation in the 2006 Immigration Protest Rallies." *Urban Affairs Review* 44(5):736–764.

Berryman, Phillip. 1984. *The Religious Roots of Rebellion: Christians in Central American Revolutions*. Maryknoll, NY: Orbis Books.

Bourdieu, Pierre. 1997. "The Forms of Capital." In *Education, Culture, Economy, and Society*, edited by A. H. Halsey, Hugh Lauder, Phillip Brown, and Amy Stuart Wells, 46–58. Oxford: Oxford University Press.

Bourdieu, Pierre, and Jean-Claude Passeron. 1977. *Reproduction in Education, Culture and Society*. London: Sage.

Braunstein, Ruth. 2017. *Prophets and Patriots: Faith in Democracy across the Political Divide*. Oakland: University of California Press, 2017.

Braunstein, Ruth, Todd Nicholas Fuist, and Rhys H. Williams, eds. 2017. *Religion and Progressive Activism: New Stories about Faith and Politics*. New York: New York University Press.

Budiman, Abby. 2020. "Key Findings about U.S. Immigrants." Pew Research Center, August 20. www.pewresearch.org.

Buergenthal, Thomas. 1994. "The United Nations Truth Commission for El Salvador." *Vanderbilt Journal of Transnational Law* 27(3):497–544.

Cadava, Geraldo L. 2013. *Standing on Common Ground*. Cambridge, MA: Harvard University Press.

Cardoso, Fernando Henrique, and Enzo Faletto. 1979. *Dependency and Development in Latin América*. Berkeley: University of California Press.

Charles, Mark, and Soong-Chan Rah. 2019. *Unsettling Truths: The Ongoing, Dehumanizing Legacy of the Doctrine of Discovery*. Downers Grove, IL: Intervarsity Press.

Chinchilla, Norma Stoltz, Nora Hamilton, and James Loucky. 2009. "The Sanctuary Movement and Central American Activism in Los Angeles." *Latin American Perspectives* 36(6):101–126.

Christerson, Brad, Korie L. Edwards, and Michael O. Emerson. 2005. *Against All Odds: The Struggle for Racial Integration in Religious Organizations.* New York: New York University Press.

Cobb, Ryon J., Samuel L. Perry, and Kevin D. Dougherty. 2015. "United by Faith? Race/Ethnicity, Congregational Diversity, and Explanations of Racial Inequality." *Sociology of Religion* 76(2):177–198.

Cooperman, Alan. 2006. "Letter on Immigration Deepens Split among Evangelicals." *Washington Post*, April 5.

Crandall, Britta H., and Russell C. Crandall. 2021. *"Our Hemisphere"? The United States in Latin America, from 1776 to the Twenty-First Century.* New Haven, CT: Yale University Press.

Cunningham, Hilary. 1995. *God and Caesar at the Rio Grande: Sanctuary and the Politics of Religion.* Minneapolis: University of Minnesota Press.

Department of Homeland Security. 2016. "Fiscal Year 2016 ICE Enforcement and Removal Operations Report." www.ice.gov.

———. 2019a. "U.S. Immigration and Customs Enforcement Fiscal Year 2019 Enforcement and Removal Operations Report." www.ice.gov.

———. 2019b. "Concerns about ICE Detainee Treatment and Care at Four Detention Facilities." Document OIG-19-47. www.oig.dhs.gov.

Diaz-Edelman, Mia. 2017. "Activist Etiquette in the Multicultural Immigrant Rights Movement." In *Religion and Progressive Activism: New Stories about Faith and Politics*, edited by Ruth Braunstein, Todd Nicholas Fuist, and Rhys H. Williams, 138–160. New York: New York University Press.

Domhoff, G. William. 2013. *Who Rules America? The Triumph of the Corporate Rich.* 7th ed. New York: McGraw-Hill.

Dougherty, Kevin D., and Kimberly R. Huyser. 2008. "Racially Diverse Congregations: Organizational Identity and the Accommodation of Differences." *Journal for the Scientific Study of Religion* 47(1):23–43.

Eagly, Ingrid, and Steven Shafer. 2016. "Access to Counsel in Immigration Court." Special report to the American Immigration Council. www.americanimmigrationcouncil.org.

Edwards, Korie L. 2008. *The Elusive Dream: The Power of Race in Interracial Churches.* New York: Oxford University Press.

Edwards, Korie L., Brad Christerson, and Michael O. Emerson. 2013. "Race, Religious Organizations, and Integration." *Annual Review of Sociology* 39(1):211–28.

Emerson, Michael O., and Glen Bracey. 2024. *The Religion of Whiteness: How Race Distorts Christian Faith.* New York: Oxford University Press.

Emerson, Michael O., and Christian Smith. 2000. *Divided by Faith: Evangelical Religion and the Problem of Race in America.* New York: Oxford University Press.

Espinosa, Gaston. 2016. *Latino Pentecostals in America: Faith and Politics in Action.* Cambridge, MA: Harvard University Press.

Executive Order 13768. 2017, January 25. *Federal Register* 82(18):8799–8803. www.govinfo.gov.

Fife, John. 2008, July. Interview with Alexia Salvatierra.

Finke, Roger, and Rodney Stark. 1992. *The Churching of America, 1776–1990: Winners and Losers in our Religious Economy.* New Brunswick, NJ: Rutgers University Press.

Flory, Richard, Brie Loskota, and Donald Miller. 2011. "Forging a New Moral and Political Agenda: The Civic Role of Religion in Los Angeles, 1992–2010." Los Angeles: University of Southern California, Center for Religion and Civic Culture. https://crcc.usc.edu.

García, María Cristina. 2006. *Seeking Refuge: Central American Migration to Mexico, the United States, and Canada.* Berkeley: University of California Press.

García, Mario T. 2008. *Católicos: Resistance and Affirmation in Chicano Catholic History.* Austin: University of Texas Press.

———. 2018. *Father Luis Olivares, a Biography: Faith Politics and the Origins of the Sanctuary Movement in Los Angeles.* Chapel Hill: University of North Carolina Press.

Gilens, Martin, and Benjamin I. Page. 2014. "Testing Theories of American Politics: Elites, Interest Groups, and Average Citizens." *Perspectives on Politics* 12(3):564–581.

Gomez, Medardo. 2013, October. Interview with Alexia Salvatierra.

Gonzalez, Daniel. 2020. "628 Parents of Separated Children Are Still Missing. Here's Why Immigrant Advocates Can't Find Them." *USA Today*, December 11. www.usatoday.com.

Goodwin, Jeff, and James M. Jasper, eds. 2014. *The Social Movements Reader: Cases and Concepts.* 3rd ed. West Sussex, UK: Wiley-Blackwell.

Haag, Matthew. 2019. "Thousands of Immigrant Children Said They Were Sexually Abused in U.S. Detention Centers, Report Says." *New York Times*, February 27. www.nytimes.com.

Hillar, Marian. 1993. "Liberation Theology: Religious Response to Social Problems. A Survey." In *Humanism and Social Issues: Anthology of Essays*, edited by Marian Hillar and H. Richard Leuchtag. Houston: Humanists Involved in Greater Houston.

Himes, Thomas. 2010. "Protests Spur Baldwin Park City Council to Suspend All Checkpoints." *Whittier Daily News*, August 5. www.whittierdailynews.com.

Hoefer, Michael, Nancy Rytina, and Christopher Campbell. 2006. "Estimates of the Unauthorized Immigrant Population Residing in the United States: January 2006." *Population Estimates*, August. Department of Homeland Security, Office of Immigration Statistics, Policy Directorate. www.dhs.gov.

Hondagneu-Sotelo, Pierrette. 2008. *God's Heart Has No Borders.* Berkeley: University of California Press.

Immigration and Customs Enforcement. 2010. "Memorandum for All ICE Employees." www.ice.gov.

Kendi, Ibram X. 2017. *Stamped from the Beginning: A Definitive History of Racist Ideas.* New York: Nation Books.

Krogstad, Jens Manuel, and Mark Hugo Lopez. 2021. "Most Latinos Say U.S. Immigration System Needs Big Changes." Pew Research Center, April 20. www.pewresearch.org.

Lambelet, Kyle B. T. 2019. *¡Presente!: Nonviolent Politics and the Resurrection of the Dead*. Washington, DC: Georgetown University Press.

La Tour, Jesse. 2018. "Fullerton Will Not Join Lawsuit Against State." *Fullerton Observer* 40(7):1–2.

Levine, Daniel. 1992. *Popular Voices in Latin American Catholicism*. Princeton, NJ: Princeton University Press.

Longfield, Bradley. 1991. *The Presbyterian Controversy: Fundamentalists, Modernists, and Moderates*. New York: Oxford University Press.

Lorentzen, Robin. 1991. *Women in the Sanctuary Movement*. Philadelphia: Temple University Press.

Ludden, Jennifer. 2007. "Polls, Interest Groups Disagree on Immigration Bill." National Public Radio. www.npr.org.

Marsden, George. 2006. *Fundamentalism and American Culture*. 2nd ed. New York: Oxford University Press.

Marsh, Charles. 2006. *The Beloved Community: How Faith Shapes Social Justice from the Civil Rights Movement to Today*. New York: Basic Books.

Martinez, Arlene. 2019. "ICE Detention Centers Rife with Abuse, Investigation Finds." *USA Today*, December 23. www.usatoday.com.

Martinez, Juan. 2018. *The Story of Latino Protestants in the United States*. Grand Rapids, MI: Eerdmans.

Martinez, Richard Edward. 2010. *PADRES: The National Chicano Priest Movement*. Austin: University of Texas Press.

Matos, Yalidy. 2021. "The 'American DREAM': Understanding White Americans' Support for the DREAM Act and Punitive Immigration Policies." *Perspectives on Politics* 19(2):422–441.

McAdam, Doug. 1982. *Political Process and the Development of the Black Insurgency, 1930–1970*. Chicago: University of Chicago Press.

Medina, Lara. 2004. *Las Hermanas: Chicana/Latina Religious-Political Activism in the U.S. Catholic Church*. Philadelphia: Temple University Press.

Melkonian-Hoover, Ruth, and Lyman A. Kellstedt. 2019. *Evangelicals and Immigration: Fault Lines among the Faithful*. Cham, Switzerland: Palgrave Harcourt.

Miller, Donald. 1997. *Reinventing American Protestantism: Christianity in the New Millennium*. Berkeley: University of California Press.

Moberg, David. 2006. *The Great Reversal: Reconciling Evangelism and Social Concern*. Eugene, OR: Wipf and Stock.

Morris, Aldon D. 1984. *The Origins of the Civil Rights Movement: Black Communities Organizing for Change*. New York: Free Press.

Mulder, Mark, Aida I. Ramos, and Gerardo Marti. 2017. *Latino Protestants in America: Growing and Diverse*. Lanham, MD: Rowman & Littlefield.

National Immigration Forum. n.d. www.immigrationforum.org.

National Opinion Research Center. 2021. "General Social Survey." Chicago: University of Chicago, National Opinion Research Center. https://gssdataexplorer.norc.org.

Park, Julie, Jude Paul Matias Dizon, and Moya Malcolm. 2019. "Spiritual Capital in Communities of Color: Religion and Spirituality as Sources of Community Cultural Wealth." *Urban Review* 52:127–150.

Pérez Huber, Lindsay. 2009. "Challenging Racist Nativist Framing: Acknowledging the Community Cultural Wealth of Undocumented Chicana College Students to Reframe the Immigration Debate." *Harvard Educational Review* 79(4):704–730.

Pew Research Center. 2014. "The Shifting Religious Identity of Latinos in the United States." May 7. www.pewresearch.org.

Pierce, Sarah, and Jessica Bolter. 2020. "Dismantling and Reconstructing the U.S. Immigration System: A Catalog of Changes under the Trump Presidency." Migration Policy Institute, July. www.migrationpolicy.org.

Portes, Alejandro. 1998. "Social Capital: Its Origins and Applications in Modern Sociology." *Annual Review of Sociology* 24:1–25.

Putnam, Robert. 2000. *Bowling Alone: The Collapse and Revival of American Community*. New York: Simon & Schuster.

Reed, Jean-Pierre, and Warren S. Goldstein. 2022. "An Introduction to the Critical Study of Religion in Rebellions, Revolutions, and Social Movements." In *Religion in Rebellions, Revolutions, and Social Movements*, edited by Warren S. Goldstein and Jean-Pierre Reed, 1–28. London: Routledge.

Romero, Oscar. 2004. *The Violence of Love*. Maryknoll, NY: Orbis Books.

Romero, Robert Chao. 2016. "Migration as Grace." *International Journal of Urban Transformation* 1:11–30.

———. 2020. *Brown Church: Five Centuries of Latina/o Social Justice, Theology and Identity*. Downers Grove, IL: Intervarsity Press.

Rothenberg, Daniel. 2016. *Memory of Silence: The Guatemalan Truth Commission Report*. London: Palgrave Macmillan.

Salvatierra, Alexia, and Peter Heltzel. 2014. *Faith-Rooted Organizing: Mobilizing the Church in Service to the World*. Downers Grove, IL: Intervarsity Press.

Salvatierra, Alexia, and Brandon Wrencher. 2022. *Buried Seeds: Learning from the Vibrant Resiliency of Marginalized Christian Communities*. Ada, MI: Baker Academic Press.

Sherman, Christopher, Martha Mendoza, and Garance Burke. 2019. "US Held Record Number of Migrant Children in Custody in 2019." Associated Press, November 12. www.apnews.com.

Sieff, Kevin, and Sarah Kinosian. 2019. "29 Parents Separated from Their Children and Deported Last Year Arrive at U.S. Border to Request Asylum." *Los Angeles Times*, March 2.

Soerens, Matthew, and Jenny Hwang. 2009. *Welcoming the Stranger: Justice, Compassion, and Truth in the Immigration Debate*. Downers Grove, IL: Intervarsity Press.

Tisby, Jamar. 2019. *The Color of Compromise: The Truth about the American Church's Complicity in Racism*. Grand Rapids, MI: Zondervan.

Tombs, David. 2002. *Latin American Liberation Theology*. Boston: Brill.

Weber, Max. 1978. *Economy and Society*. 2 vols. Berkeley: University of California Press.

Whitehead, Andrew L., and Samuel L. Perry. 2020. *Taking America Back for God: Christian Nationalism in the United States*. New York: Oxford University Press.

Wood, Richard. 2002. *Faith in Action: Religion, Race and Democratic Organizing in America*. Chicago: University of Chicago Press.

Yosso, Tara J. 2005. "Whose Culture Has Capital? A Critical Race Theory Discussion of Community Cultural Wealth." *Race Ethnicity and Education* 8(1):69–91.

Yukich, Grace. 2013. *One Family Under God: Immigration Politics and Progressive Religion in America*. New York: Oxford University Press.

INDEX

ABOUT THE AUTHORS

BRAD CHRISTERSON is Professor in the Department of Sociology at Biola University and co-author of *The Rise of Network Christianity, Growing Up in America: The Power of Race in the Lives of Teens,* and *Against All Odds: The Struggle for Racial Integration in Religious Organizations.*

ALEXIA SALVATIERRA is Academic Dean of the Centro Latino and Associate Professor of Mission and Global Transformation at Fuller Theological Seminary and co-author of *Buried Seeds: Learning from the Vibrant Resiliency of Marginalized Christian Communities.*

ROBERT CHAO ROMERO is Associate Professor in the Department of Chicana/o and Central American Studies at the University of California, Los Angeles. He is the author of several books, including *The Chinese in Mexico, 1882–1940* and *Brown Church: Five Centuries of Latina/o Social Justice, Theology, and Identity.*

NANCY WANG YUEN is a Diversity, Equity, Inclusion and Belonging (DEIB) consultant for Peoplism and author of *Reel Inequality: Hollywood Actors and Racism.*

Milton Keynes UK
Ingram Content Group UK Ltd.
UKHW012318111023
430419UK00007B/446

9 781479 816422